Unleash Your Moxie

A Girl's Guide to Becoming

Fiercely **Bold**,

Incredibly **Happy**,

and Practically **Superhuman**!

CRYSTAL O'CONNOR

DEDICATION

To my children; I love you to the moon and back.

To my grandmother Janice; you inspire me.

To every woman who dreams of having an
extraordinary life.

To my friend Sarah; you define unconditional love.

CONTENTS

ACKNOWLEDGMENTS

Many thanks and much appreciation to many people: Melissa Lamming, who started out as a client and turned into a surrogate sister – your Moxie, expertise, and skills inspire me every day. Your ability to tackle projects with dedication and detail helped bring this book to fruition. John Lamming, for your patience and help in assembling and editing this book to perfection. Sarah and Woody Wilson, for being there for me like family. Barbara Corcoran, for inspiring me to be brave and to swim with the sharks. Cactus Jack, for just being you, a true entrepreneur, and showing me how it's done! My clients – teaching you has taught me more. You are the reason for this book, and the wind beneath my wings. My fourth grade teacher, Sister Marie Celine and my two aunts, Sister Cecile and Sister Consuela – your efforts were never in vain. Thank you for caring enough to devote your life to teaching discipline, resilience, and Moxie ...without ever resorting to physical force.

Make sure to visit _www.MoxieU.com_ for bonuses I give subscribers, and for a regular dose of Moxie Inspiration.

FOREWORD

Unleash Your Moxie is a must-read for anyone looking to really make explosive changes in their life. I've worked with thousands of entrepreneurs across the world, and I'd tell all of them to read it and "get Moxie," just like Crystal says. Crystal emulates the Moxie spirit, and how she's grown her business out of thin air proves my theory that you must have the YES! energy.

Trust me, she will wake up and shake up your life. She's got that "it" factor – energy that could fill a banquet hall! Her book offers inner wisdom and ignites your mind to make substantial positive life changes – as soon as you read it! She's a raw, honest, truth-teller, straight up. Her stories of overcoming obstacles on her personal journey are not just awe-inspiring, but will leave you supercharged and ready to take ownership of your life. It's about time someone wrote a book about the power of self-talk, faith, and self-worth the way Crystal O'Connor does in *Unleash Your Moxie*.

Just starting and having that "move forward no matter what" attitude is what creates magic and solutions. All problems have solutions. Crystal knows this and it's what helps her tap into what we call God and Spirit source. Crystal shares her personal struggles and stories of getting knocked down, and how building up a life and business around those "hits" can practically serve as an advantage. It's just all about how you perceive it. It's your attitude.

Just like me, Crystal is a mother who believes in the human spirit's potential and in teaching her kids what being financially free means: what it takes and how to do it step by step. She doesn't just talk the talk, but walks it too. She knows that when you motivate people with words, you can inspire them to take action, but when you show them and teach them systematically, you change the entire family's "wealth legacy."

She knows that it's about taking action NOW and not putting things off until it's comfortable. Big, audacious goals are achieved when you take action when it's least comfortable. She knows you can get anything and everything you want with God, faith, and action. That's what "Moxie" is – it's faith in action.

Everyone wins when you take forward action in faith and do what you were meant to do. Letting go of fear, worry, and procrastination, and fighting your own inner resistance is a formula for success. My friend and mentor Bob Proctor puts it well; he says, "This vibration accounts for the difference between mind and matter, between the physical and the nonphysical worlds."

It's finding that happy place where you know when to surrender and you know when to push forward with determination. It's not always about working too hard, either, because many times working too hard just means you're spinning your wheels and you need to get the help from those who have skills you don't. We don't have to have all the answers; we just need to know that there are others out there who do.

And this is the Moxie that is required – the energy that equates to "Yes I can and yes I will."

Loral Langemeier
Five-time New York Times and Wall Street Journal
best-selling author and money expert

www.liveoutloud.com

Getting Moxie

Getting Moxie

This is a life skills guide for women and smart men who get in their own way on their journey to getting what they want. It's meant to be a healthy dose of unusual advice with a twist of humor. It's not for those who want to stay meek, struggling, or dependent on others. It's for those "nice gals" who feel a rumbling deep in their souls and know they want more… but need to be pushed a little. This guide is for those of you who know you were meant for bigger things – those who've been through hell and want permission to raise a little too. It's not for those who've convinced themselves that money is evil, that being broke is somehow noble, or that being humble means staying in bad relationships. It's for those who want clarity and need to be lifted out of their crap with a jolt of reality.

You may laugh. You may cry. You may just decide to transform your entire life. If my personal stories help you in any way feel stronger, that is what I've included them for. Let my mess be a message to you that you can start over after falling down – you can feel defeated, humiliated, unappreciated, and unfulfilled, and simply decide to turn it all around in the blink of an eye. It all depends on you and what you want in life.

I started out writing a business book, and in the process realized that business and mindset are intertwined. *So,* you may ask, *why did you write this book and what the hell is Moxie anyway?* Well, I wrote this book because I hate being told what to do, and I love freedom. I decided to be an entrepreneur and I think you should too. Why live life loathing what you do, day in and day out, dragging through your days in agony – or worse, apathy?

Webster's defines *moxie* as "energy, pep, courage, determination and know-how," and I feel we could all use a little more of it. A big dose of it certainly helped me.

I wasn't born knowing I had it; I had to tap into it. I want to share with you how you can acquire it and use it to take the world by storm. I want you to start living the life you were meant to live, free of the dreads, fears, worries, and angst that stop you from living large.

Sometimes people confuse being Moxie with being a bitch. They are not the same. The truth is that our fear of the word "bitch" makes us weak, confused, and fearful – we women, mainly. This fear of being a "bitch" is what's holding you back from almost everything you can't seem to get your hands on. Don't let your feelings about the word "bitch" hold you back from being Moxie.

There really never is any need to be mean, rude, crass, or belligerent toward anyone. You can get what you want without busting someone's balls or telling anyone off. In fact, this book may just help you discover the art of telling someone to go to hell, and having them thank you for it. They may never know exactly what you did or how you did it... but you'll not be seen as a bitch by anyone you care about.

Let me introduce you to Moxie in a way that will help you embrace the word.

Meet Moxie

Moxie wakes up every day with a plan and won't compromise what she wants to make others happy. She understands that when she gets what she wants, it makes everyone around her happy too. She understands that sacrifice doesn't mean letting herself go, working at a job she hates, or remaining stuck in a relationship that is sucking the life out of her. She knows it doesn't mean feeling devalued, unappreciated, and underpaid. She knows that saying "No" to what she doesn't want to do gives her time to do what she does, and she doesn't let guilt etch itself into her soul like a bad tattoo, a constant reminder of "that stupid night."

She learns from her mistakes and moves on. She forgives but does not forget, and never makes the same mistake twice. She forges ahead when she can't see the light at the end of the tunnel because she has faith in herself. Even though Mom or Grandma may have done things a certain way, she understands that times have changed, and that she's part of that shift.

Moxie doesn't let regret screw with her mind or send her into the "poor-me" zone. She never looks back to find herself blaming anyone – this guy, that woman, or the dreadful boss that screwed it all up for her and got in her way. She has a very real and powerful sense of personal responsibility. She knows that everything she ever wants is at her fingertips – all she needs is a plan.

Moxie has X-ray vision and sees through the crap people dish out. She knows that hurting people hurt others, and she doesn't take things too personally. She bolts when she's not being treated the way she wants, but she does it with grace.

She's not a cling-on; she knows how to attract everything she wants, and never resorts to playing games. (Her opponents wouldn't have a chance anyway.) She's razor sharp, and isn't afraid to negotiate for fear of losing a deal – she knows there are other deals out there. She doesn't act out of fear; she acts in spite of it. She flies below the radar at just the right times. She's never boastful, competitive, or conceited. People notice her wit, and it's her results themselves that demand attention.

How Moxie Works

I came to know how Moxie works over years of screwing up, broken sacred boundaries, tearful revelations, screaming fits of rage and regret, and miraculous moments in which the truth was revealed – the truth that we are not alone and there is a God or higher power watching over us, although our free will is ultimately what is attracting or resisting what we want.

This is meant to be a girl's guide – advice and wisdom about when to shut up and when to speak up, and how to feel confident enough to use the laws of the universe and the laws of scalability to grow good fortune in every corner of life. To grow beyond limits, to capture big dreams otherwise lost, to rise above mediocrity, and to break the chains of regret and limiting beliefs. To grow thicker skin and shed what's not allowing the good stuff in.

Moxie listens to her own inner self. She's not just talking her talk, she's walking it too. She knows God gave her a compass, and she won't ignore it anymore. Her gut, her intuition, is speaking to her, like a guide – telling her when to let go, when to forge ahead, and when to allow God to steer and depend on faith.

Moxie is Faith in Action

We don't talk enough about faith: what it is and what it really means, how powerful it can be, and the magic it can create all around us.

Without faith we have very little. We have aimless wandering, random uncertainty, mindless direction, desperate needy spirits, and half-assed attempts at everything.

We see it all around us: People starting businesses, only to give up way too soon. People attempting to lose weight without realizing that faith and belief is what breaks the bad habits of crappy eating and a sedentary lifestyle. People depending on the government to feed them and their families because they don't have the faith to start a million-dollar business – even though they are perfectly capable of doing so. Faith is the one thing that has led me to every trick I've ever pulled out of my hat.

It's like magic. Yes. God and faith mixed with Moxie is like magic. This book is about taking action. It's not just another theory that pumps up your spirits and results in nothing.

Moxie Manifests What She Wants

You can manifest anything. I've manifested babies, money, angels… and a whole lot of crap that just about ripped the soul right out of me. I've been on my knees begging for mercy. I've been hit in the face so hard my neck needed to be X-rayed. I've seen my life flash before my eyes in a head on collision. I've watched a man die right before me. I've been a homeless teen, endured physical and mental abuse by loved ones, and been eight minutes away from pulling the trigger and calling it all off. I've lost loved ones, tragically, when it could have been prevented. I've witnessed coincidences that would blow your mind. I've been attacked in a parking lot by a gang, and I know how to take a hit and get back up. I've given birth on the floor of my own bedroom. I've attracted miracles beyond imagining. I believe anyone can do it, and I want to help you begin to do it too.

Everything your heart desires, you can have. You can place any order, but you've got to be ready for the outcome and realize it will come in the form of an opportunity. When it appears, you have to say yes. You have to be Moxie enough to grab it. You have to open your eyes and see that it's right there… and to realize that nothing is pure take – you've got to give a little too.

You want the fairy tale? You want the million dollar house? You want to go on trips around the world feeding the hungry? You want a baby? I can tell you how to get them. (I manifested three babies in two years!)

Pick your fantasy – I know how to manifest it. Nothing is delusional or impossible …unless you just sit there.

No, I'm not claiming to be the Second Coming. I *am* claiming to know how to tap into something He provided for us. And I can promise that miracles *can* happen after you get your mindset right and discover how resilient, bold, clever, and intentional you can be.

Let go of your ego, your flakiness, your insecurities, your greed, your jealousies, your limiting beliefs about what you can do, your sad story, your victim mentality, those crappy limiting belief systems, that stupid word "**can't**," and realize that you **can**.

The word "can't" pisses me off. It's a word we let someone bury in our subconscious when we were kids, sucking our thumbs. We gave up sucking our thumbs, but never gave up that word.

Faith is something we create, and it looks a lot like luck. Want to be that lucky bitch you've always envied? The one who seems to get everything she ever wanted and makes things look easy? Stock up on faith – you'll get nowhere without it.

The craziest thing I've ever seen is swarms of people thumping their Bibles and at the same time receiving benefits provided by the government. That's not faith. That's Crazy Town.

You want everything your heart desires? You will need one ingredient. It's called Moxie, and anyone can get it. Moxie is faith in action. Want to learn how to get some? Read on.

Here we go. Let's do this.

Our Dreams Die of Shame

If you want to make bank in business you've got to get over yourself. Too many people are afraid to look stupid, ridiculous, or odd – afraid of being humiliated or rejected. This is a formula for death.

Our dreams die of shame if we let them. I see it every day. People too proud to work hard, too proud to ask for the sale, too proud to look different... This pride is rooted in fear and it's a sure way to lose. It's the girl who's willing to try something different – willing to start at 1.0 and work up to 4.0 – who earns the keys to the kingdom.

The woman who finally decides she's not going to settle, who takes the leap and instead markets herself, tells her story, and holds that free tele-class – she's the one who has the $10k+ months. It's the woman willing to hear the words "No thanks" over and over and keep going who earns the fancy car and the Chanel purse. This girl realizes that leading an unconventional life can be threatening to others, but she does it anyway because that's her dream. She knows that she is never alone when she's her own best friend.

Want to succeed in business? Get to know marketing and sales. Be bold enough to peel away the shame and get a little metaphorically naked. Learn how to deal.

Get Comfortable With Being Uncomfortable

"You gain strength, courage and confidence by every experience in which you really stop and look fear in the face. You must do the thing you think you cannot do."

Eleanor Roosevelt

People are way too comfortable. We are comfort addicts. Want to get what you want? Get uncomfortable and get used to it. We've all heard "no pain, no gain," right? Well, let me tell you something. Sitting around watching TV is comfortable, reading novels is comfortable, eating cake is comfortable, and getting an epidural is comfortable. Saying this is not going to make me popular, but women were not meant to get epidurals. We are tough. We are super resilient. Think about it: We are capable of pushing out 8-10 pound human beings from the most intimate and sensitive parts of our bodies and live to tell about it.

I'll admit I eat cake. I've eaten a lot of cake in my life. It's my favorite comfort food. I want to eat it every single day. I know though that if I did I'd be wearing it on my ass soon after. I know that if I watch too much TV the same thing will happen. I've decided having a fat ass is not comfortable so I don't eat cake every day and I limit TV to a couple of hours a week, if that.

I used to hate hard work. I hated it as a kid but I did it. I hated that I had to clean the crazy lady's house down the street on

Saturdays for four hours to make a few bucks, while my friends were playing outside. You know what, though? It showed me what that hard work turned into. It turned into opportunities. It earned me the money to buy things. But mostly it taught me at a young age that I didn't want to clean houses. It helped me value my time better and realize that being paid by the hour sucks. It's probably what led me to leave my teaching career for an outside sales executive position.

I enjoyed the freedom. I loved the money. But I hated selling. So I made a game of it. I taught myself how to sell. Repetition and the fact that I hated being rejected also taught me how to sell better. Being rejected is very uncomfortable, so I learned how to sell to avoid rejection. I overcame it by facing it and flipping it. I could either leave (and get paid by-the-hour wages or crappy teacher's pay) or learn how to sell. I absolutely love to teach but I want to teach on my own terms. I've learned that I can still teach while living the life I want.

I actually started selling when I was in the first grade... and you likely did too. I sold Christmas cards door to door to make money for Christmas gifts. I was always finding something to sell and realized that it's all in the numbers. I wasn't as afraid back then, either. It was going to be more uncomfortable for me to not have money for Christmas gifts than it was to get rejected trying to sell. I'd count houses and realize that if I needed to sell a certain number of cards, I'd need to get rejected by a certain number of houses. I also realized that in all these houses, I was bound to find at least one buyer, which meant facing rejection with a whole new attitude. I made a game of it. Making a game of it, rewarding yourself, and accepting the uncomfortable parts will always promote growth. It's just inevitable.

In sales I had to drive or travel to most of my sales appointments. I made a game of the process so that I could meet my weekly sales goals. I would allow myself to stop once I was either rejected 15 times or had made a certain amount in sales. It's all habits. We either create a habit of comfort and mediocrity, or we make a habit of pushing through the fear and growing from it. I believe without a doubt that anything and everything can become a habit. We choose which habits we make our own.

I have an aunt who has never driven more than 30 miles by herself. This is a fear of hers. It has stopped her from expanding in so many areas of her life. That may sound ridiculous to some of you, but big fears and common fears hold us back in similar ways. It's not just the fact that a fear is silly or unusual; it's the fact that we become habitual in avoiding it …until we get fed up with it and realize it's leading us to live a miserable, mediocre life.

When you face uncomfortable situations head-on every day, you get Moxie. Start by facing little fears. Make a game of it. Make a list of fears, big and small, and slowly begin to face them and mark them off one by one. This is how you begin to change your life: one fear at a time.

Burn the Ships

How bad do you want something? I suggest you burn the ships to get it.

In Napoleon Hill's book *Think and Grow Rich*, he shares the story of the world's greatest empire builder, Alexander the Great, who burned his boats upon arrival on the shores of Persia. By burning his boats, "Alex" committed his men to victory over the Persians, who far outnumbered them. At the time, Persia also had the most powerful naval fleet in the world. Considering what Alex was facing, the decision to destroy the Greeks' only hope of retreat was extraordinary. Nonetheless, it proved to be correct.

Our history books are full of other fearless commanders who used the same strategy to guarantee victory. Taric el Tuerto, otherwise known as Tariq ibn Ziyad, the general who conquered Hispania in 711, burned his boats when fighting the Spaniards. He too had a valid reason to do so: his army was outnumbered five to one.

If you've made a bad habit your whole life of giving up each and every time you have set out to achieve something big, you really need to seriously consider taking this approach. It will eradicate any possibility of retreat from your mind, and commit you to victory. Don't let defeat be an option.

Get an accountability partner. Set things up so that you *have* to arrive at your destination. Be relentless. Be unwavering. Stay committed. Have no exit strategy. No giving up. No giving in. No accepting less than what you set out to achieve.

It works for me. Sometimes the best thing you can do to get the result you want is to burn the ships yourself.

A common fear is speaking in front of groups of people. If this is one of your fears, write it down. You don't have to face it tomorrow or anything, but if you're like me and want to get it over with, by all means don't let me stop you.

Barbara Corcoran, of the hit TV show *Shark Tank* and author of *Shark Tales: How I Turned $1,000 into a Billion Dollar Business*, tells the story of how she was asked to be a keynote speaker for the first time and address a thousand executives at a dinner banquet. She said yes, with no experience. She bombed the speech and, embarrassed as she was, she used that experience and grew from it. She studied public speaking and signed up to teach a real estate class. As it turned out, this didn't just give her sharper speaking skills; it put her in front of some pretty savvy real estate agents with serious connections, who helped her grow her real estate agency.

Sometimes facing hurdles with bravery and humility and a willingness to grow can catapult us to success.

If you want to run a marathon, just show up. Don't let quitting be an option. Just start, and odds are you'll finish. You'll have better luck if you train for it – I promise you that – but you get the point.

If you have a fear of snakes or spiders, go find one. Suck it up and decide to touch it or hold it. Realize that it's not that big a deal. If you're afraid of driving long distances by yourself, plan a trip 100 to 300 miles away all by your Moxie self, and check it off your list.

When you want something with a white hot desire or passion, **burn the ships** and just decide that retreating is not an option. It's a sure way to manifest what you want.

Burning the ships creates intention and direction. When you do this, not only does something amazing happen to you and your energy level, but somehow the universe works with you and creates a path for you. Things begin to shift. You begin to see clearly the outcome you desire, and things begin to line up as if by magic. This is when bizarre coincidences start to occur. The right people show up. Clients hire you from out of the blue. You get a $40k sale on what started out as an ordinary day. Luck starts dropping things in your lap, and you begin to feel like a magician.

We Attract What We Feel

When you prove your desire and your belief, you will win ten times over. I promise you. Sometimes we have built up so much negative self-talk, so much doubting, that we have literally taught ourselves to fail.

We all do this. We do it every day. The solution is to become very aware of your inner chatter on a daily basis. Ask yourself, "Am I letting in what I really want, or am I resisting with worry, disbelief, and visions of failure?"

> *"Ask and it will be given to you; seek and you will find; knock and the door will be opened to you."*
>
> Matthew 7:7

> *"If you believe, you will receive whatever you ask for in prayer."*
>
> Matthew 21:22

Ask yourself if you are actually preventing your desires and dreams from coming true and sabotaging your own efforts by not fully believing.

Change your self-talk. Write down your specific requests repeatedly. Feel what it would be like to have that thing you want — that baby, that experience, that job, that house. Whatever your heart's desire, I'm convinced God wants you to have it. Know, with all your heart, that what you want is on its way.

"Acting as if" is one of the hardest things to do, but there is very real power in it. When you do this, you create pathways to answers and opportunities that seem like bizarre coincidences or sheer luck. You create magnetic energy that will attract the people, circumstances, and experiences that will provide you with what you desire.

You do not need to know **how** it will happen. You only need to be specific about the desire. Let God and the Universe decide how it will come to fruition.

When I started my first real business, a nanny agency, I had a lot of issues with it. That's likely why it didn't work out. I was terrified of being responsible for the kids that I placed with the nannies. I would interview the nannies personally, and always ran background checks on them. But after I'd placed them, I would begin to imagine them doing terrible things, like leaving the child unattended. I'd have outlandish thoughts that would keep me up at night. I would work myself up, expecting something to go wrong.

I'd change my mind at the last minute, cancel the service request to the nanny, and show up myself to do the job. I totally sabotaged my business and finally realized I just didn't have the nerves to deal with it.

This is an example of fear based thinking and fear based decision making. Fear never wins us our heart's desires. Fear is rooted in doubt. Doubt and worry are our worst enemies.

I eventually decided I would work as a nanny broker and find nannies for agencies in New York. I became paranoid that the agencies wouldn't pay me the fees, and wound up attracting it. In fact, several times I wasn't paid the fees and it was my own fault. I eventually gave up and walked away, thinking I had been defeated. I felt taken advantage of, betrayed, and victimized. With nothing positive to move me forward, I gave up. I felt like a failure. It wasn't that I was a failure – I just needed to adjust my contracts, set up more productive systems, and learn how to run my business more like a business. I also needed to learn marketing, because back then I had no real experience with marketing and no idea how to market in that industry. I failed because I chose to fail. It was my own fault.

For years I watched a close family friend fret and worry about her kids. No doubt she adored them like any mom, but a lot of her decisions were fear based. I once watched her go into hysterics when she saw her son choking on food at the dinner table. I watched her scream and panic when she thought her son was drowning in the pool. (He was only playing.) As a child, I was mystified by this. One night, she was up late listening to the police scanner, and heard that her son had been in a car accident in his brand new car. She worked herself into such a panic that they had to call her an ambulance. Her son was rushed to the hospital still alive, but while the paramedics were putting him on the stretcher they failed to turn him over fast enough when he said he was going to be sick to his stomach. He choked and went into cardiac arrest. While he was in a coma, she refused to go to his bedside because she could not handle seeing him in that condition. She was in constant turmoil, expecting the worst. He died five days later.

I don't mean to blame his death on her. That would be ludicrous. However, her whole life was consumed by thoughts of something bad happening. She told her friends about it. She panicked and created fearful, unhealthy energy, and I think she almost believed that she really would lose one of her children. And she did.

I knew another woman who had lost her daughter as a teenager, and who admitted to me that she always knew she would lose this youngest daughter of hers. Ever since she was born, she had this fear. That story introduced me to an idea I believe to this day. When we have a belief or a recurring thought about something, we attract it like a magnet. Sometimes we have recurring thoughts that we come to believe to be facts. Our subconscious mind stores them as truth and we come to believe our worst nightmares. How tragic. Later on, I will share more stories about my own experiences with attraction and thinking.

"Concentrate all your thoughts upon the work at hand. The sun's rays do not burn until brought to a focus."

Alexander Graham Bell

What you focus on grows, so make sure you're giving attention to what you want, or you'll attract a lot of crap that you don't.

Some people suffer from a form of self-sabotaging behavior that causes them to shut down, give up, or start another project just as they're about to wrap up the project at hand. I used to do this and you may be doing it too. I finally diagnosed it, and it has to do with feeling unworthy of completing or succeeding at something. Don't sabotage yourself just as you're about to reap the rewards of all that hard work.

I want to talk about the way you feel now. Feelings are something that we don't talk about enough, and I bet we all know a man or two who begins to squirm when you mention "feelings," right?

Well, screw that. We're here now and we're talking about it. Just you and me – let's go.

Do you wake up and feel lost? Unfulfilled? Restless? (That's me – felt that from day one!) Do you feel sad? Blue? Filled with anxiety?

These feelings mean something, and I want to help you address them.

Hope is also a feeling, and so is purpose. Feelings cause action and movement. If you feel as if you don't matter, this is not only a bunch of crap but it's a pretty crappy feeling and affects your whole system. When you feel purposeful and driven, you send out positive energy and you create that ripple effect.

It's Moxie. Trust me.

You Become Like the Five People You Spend the Most Time With

"If you're given the choice between money and sex appeal, take the money. As you get older the money will become your sex appeal."

Katherine Hepburn

I was always drawn to overachieving men. Maybe I was looking for balance or maybe I knew they'd inspire me with their drive – whatever it is, I still find myself looking for a stable-minded companion to keep me on track. What I've learned is that you do become the five people you spend the most time with. This quote has been stated in many different ways, but there is no more accurate a statement. You may think you're stronger than the pull of your peeps' influence but their ways of thinking and their habits will snatch up your dreams faster than a thief in the night if you let them... *or* they can accelerate and complement your desires, and set you on the fast path to success.

It's like osmosis, and cannot be avoided. It's just one of the laws of the universe you cannot change. Ever hear the phrase, "When you lie down with dogs, you get up with fleas?" Well, it's truth, sister.

An easy way to decide whether your tribe or five influencers in your life are helping or hindering you is by straight-up asking yourself if the five people you spend the most time with want or have the same things you want.

Think about it. Do they have the car, the family, the vision, or the house you would like to see yourself in? Do they strive for the same level of success or do they talk a big game and then spend more time watching The View and Netflix than doing the work?

What do they talk about? Do they talk about ideas or do they gossip about people? Do they share other people's dirty secrets or do they speak highly of those they want to emulate? Do they manage their time wisely? Do they care for their yards, children, and houses? You may not think this is important but it is.

Are they overweight? Do they smoke? Do they spend their money on self-help books or the latest "red room of pain" novel? Do they help their children with their homework or do they play on Facebook, chatting about nothing in particular instead? Do they spend their time arguing over politics and starting trouble wherever they go? What are they focused on? Where is their attention?

Do they listen to you when you tell them your dreams or do they laugh and give you backhanded compliments that make you feel bad?

It Takes as Much Effort to Fail as to Succeed

"It takes just as much effort to fail as it does to succeed. Life shrinks or expands in proportion to one's courage."

Anaïs Nin

As an online business and marketing coach working with small businesses, I have witnessed people put more effort into failing, giving up, or quitting than succeeding. It has been fascinating yet frustrating. It is as if we each have a thermostat set in our heads that determines the amount of income we can earn. When we hit a certain amount of income or revenue, our thermostat begins to create barriers, obstacles, and limits within us. These barriers and obstacles look rational and completely legitimate. They almost never are, though. In fact, they are illusions, created by our own subconscious minds, built of fears and limiting beliefs from our past.

I found it completely puzzling until it happened to me. More about that later – for now I'm going to share a story about a photographer I coached a few years back.

Over and over, he would begin to backtrack just as he was moments away from accomplishing bigger goals and reaching a new level of income. I watched him literally pack up and move overnight out of a 5,000 square foot studio space. It took him all night, car load after car load. He found himself able to move thousands of dollars of equipment and hundreds of pounds of furniture, computers, and lights. He even called in the "troops" (his family) to help him. They came to rescue him just as they had 20 years before when he did the same thing. His excuse was that he did it to prevent the owner of the space from taking his expensive equipment. He fired his employee and gave half his things away. But he was walking away just when he was on the brink of success.

All he needed was a few thousand dollars to avoid the problem. All he needed to do was make a few sales, put a plan together, and put the same effort into succeeding he had just put into failing.

It was baffling, but people do it all of the time. More effort put into struggling than succeeding. More time spent waffling and procrastinating than getting their Moxie on and doing what needs to get done. More effort killing themselves slowly than burning their ships to gain success.

If my son or daughter asked me in the middle of the night to come and help them move out and quit, I'd say, "No way! You're going to march in there and spend the whole day tomorrow coming up with the three grand. You're going to burn the ships, and if you can't come up with it by noon, I'm coming in and showing you where the money is, just to prove that it's easier to find the money than to give up."

I wouldn't feel bad about giving them a few reminders: "You're not a quitter. Get your head out of your ass. This is the least Moxie thing you could do."

If they still insisted on quitting I'd probably burn the ships for them. I'd show up and stand in the doorway and I'd take their car keys or studio keys. Sometimes a mom's gotta get tough.

I had noticed early on that these parents both had negative thoughts about life and issues with success. They thought they were helping their son, when really they were encouraging this same limited thinking.

To some, success is so scary that they become their own worst enemies. They say they want it, but their actions say otherwise.

Unleash Your Moxie

They lie to themselves, complain, gossip, and spend too much time watching TV. They become frustrated with themselves, and can't face the truth that's staring right at them. They spend more time and effort arguing and making up excuses than facing the truth that they are afraid of success for reasons they can't express.

It all comes down to feeling worthy or unworthy, to childhood ideas about our own capabilities. This thermostat in our heads is set to a certain familiar number we're comfortable with.

When we begin to earn more than we ever have before, we get uncomfortable. Our thermostat kicks in and shuts us down. It tells us it's getting too hot and it's time to start the self-sabotaging behavior.

We all do it. Maybe we fear gaining what we want and then losing it all. Maybe we fear the responsibility. Maybe we believe deep down that it takes more effort at the top than we can handle. We base our decisions on someone else's failures that we've witnessed. We choose to take advice from those with no experience or qualifications.

Instead we do what we know we **can** do. We run around like this photographer did, busting his ass all night, with sweat running down his brow. He knew how to fail and lie to himself, so that was what he was determined to do. To this day I've never seen such a perfect example of this truth in action. He could have made a million dollars the next day. He just needed to redirect his efforts toward the target he wanted to hit, although frankly that's exactly what he did. He wouldn't listen to advice from someone who knew what they were talking about – instead, he chose to listen to someone who didn't, because it was familiar and comfortable. He *wanted* to hit the big fat FAIL target.

Success is actually a lot easier than failure. I know what it takes for most of us to succeed. Trouble is, you can't make everyone successful or triumphant – they have to do it themselves. You can tell them exactly what to do, but they have to do it. Finding a mentor is so important because, on your way to success, you will run into mental blocks – procrastination, self-sabotage, and fears – that your mentor can spot and help you break through.

If You Feel Like an Outlaw You're On to Something Big

"If you want to study the entrepreneur, study the juvenile delinquent... The delinquent is saying with his actions, 'This sucks, I'm going to do my own thing.'"

Yvon Chouinard

I've gotten myself into hot water more times than I can count. Some of it happened because I utterly detest being told what to do. I also hate compromising or settling for anything less than what I want. When I was younger, I went to a Catholic school that had rules everywhere. My fourth grade teacher was a 72-year-old-nun. She didn't smile much and was so serious about our learning. To call her intense would be an understatement. I hated memorization and her style of teaching was all about memorizing everything. We memorized prayers, poems, long division math problems, stories, parts of the Constitution, and the Emancipation Proclamation. I got bored easily, so I rarely paid attention.

Memorization was the ultimate bore, so my attention was always elsewhere. I believe to this day that kids who get into trouble a lot in school are meant to be entrepreneurs. They need stimulation, variety, activity, movement, and excitement – but mostly the opportunity to be creative. They love creative outlets, breathing room, and complex challenges that don't require sitting for long periods of time. And the fewer rules, the better.

From the very beginning, I was drawn to other kids who got into trouble. The kids who were looking for trouble were bored and hungry for action. That was me. If there was some sort of uproar, chaos, or prank stirring things up in that school and distracting from the everyday painful dullness of the day, I was involved in it one way or another. I was letting stray animals into the school, feeding the teacher's pet's lunch to a stray dog, playing poker in the back of the room with a fellow rebel, reading a book that kids shouldn't be reading, or gluing each page corner of the teacher's manual together.

I decided that one particular day needed a little spicing up so I decided to ask permission for a rest room break. (This wasn't out of the ordinary – I was always finding ways to leave the room.) I then went out to the front of the school, took the flag down, turned it upside down, and sent it back up the pole. I didn't know that this was a national distress signal. I just thought it would be interesting to see who noticed.

Bam! It wasn't but ten minutes after I sat myself back in my chair that I heard a familiar roar. Ms. Pease, the 215-pound 8th grade Social Studies teacher, was coming down the hall toward me, yelling my name. "Crystal," she screamed at the top of her lungs, "Follow me!"

As she marched me down the hall to the office, I knew I'd hit the trouble motherlode. There stood two police officers. My immediate thought was, *What the hell does this mean?*

That was my first time feeling like an outlaw.

I made a name for myself that day and was ordered to write a three page report on respecting the flag. I was then ordered to read it aloud to each and every classroom in the school.

Since then I've become used to being the outlaw. I was made to break rules. I got comfortable with it. Yes, getting caught was humiliating, but it was necessary. It wasn't something I could control anyway. I was screaming, out of my mind with boredom, but for years no one would hear me. I didn't know what to do with my energy, my creativity, or my hunger for challenge. Acting out was my outlet.

My need to create is greater than my fear of being an outlaw. If you have ever felt restless from sitting too long and being forced to learn in an environment that just didn't work for you, you know what I'm talking about. It can really leave a kid feeling like a failure, when the truth is quite the opposite. These kids were meant to *create* the jobs for the A students – the kids who become experts in their field and thrive on consistency, repetition, and stability. There is nothing wrong with stability. I admire it, actually. I just can't do it and be happy.

I remember making up pet names for the teachers in my school who hated me the most. Sister Mary Hawkeyes, who got really good at catching me. I had to respect her – she was really good at what she did, and she kept me on my toes. It was as if she could see through walls and crowds of other children to swoop around corners and grab me just before I could launch one of my power pranks. Sister Mary Elephant couldn't move fast, and I preferred her for certain pranks. "Get in and get out" became my mantra, but with Sister Mary Elephant I had more time to be crafty.

Fast forward to today. Breaking rules, being creative, and exploring the unknown is what building a business is all about. While building my businesses from home I managed to make a mess with my ideas, and somehow had five startups going at once. I was breaking all the rules again. I wouldn't suggest it to any sane person, but I was definitely in my "Moxie zone." I loved the challenge and the act of creation, but one thing I will suggest is that you find someone to stop you from being a perpetual creator. You've got to move over into the innovation mode at some point and you can't do that by yourself with five small startups. Even Moxie can't do it, so don't kid yourself.

> *"You can have it all. You just can't have it all
> at once."*
>
> Oprah Winfrey

By "innovation mode," I mean you've got to start making money. Period. Creators need help in this area. Luckily I had 20 years of sales experience behind me and I knew what to do every time I needed to save my ass. When the bills are piling up and pressure is on, you've got to know what to do to bring home the bacon and feed the kids.

> *"Women are like tea bags, put them in hot
> water and they get stronger."*
>
> Eleanor Roosevelt

I was forced to put three of those businesses on the back burner. All kinds of problems occur when cash isn't flowing in fast enough, and you've created more work than one person can handle. I was facing a tax bill, closed bank accounts, and a repo man looking for me in the middle of night. An entire police station had it out for me because I continued to drive illegally, after three warnings, on a suspended license. When you're forced to make decisions about whether to pay the speeding ticket, the water bill, the repo man, or the web designer, it takes sharp action, quick decisions, and **faith**. There is no time or space for giving up.

It doesn't have to be this way, if you learn ahead of time how to sell. Selling and marketing is what makes every business run. Without good, solid sales and marketing, you have nothing but a hobby. Don't get me wrong. There's nothing wrong with a hobby ...as long as you don't have to pay the bills with it.

Most of my life I've felt slightly reckless. It's just how I roll. I used to hate that about myself and feel ashamed. Now I've grown to not care what others think. For years I thought something was wrong with me, and I asked myself why I couldn't be like the cautious and predictable people around me. I worked for big life insurance companies in Des Moines (the insurance capital of the world) and felt like a round peg in a square hole. I didn't know what to do with myself. In my early twenties I chose to drink and party my way through my life. I was trying to numb the pain of leading a life I was not meant to lead.

I'd wake up every morning and put on that suit like I was supposed to. I thought my only option was to be something I really wasn't. I'd park my car in the same place downtown and walk the same walk to the same office and say hi to the same people and sit at my desk taking orders from underwriters in the underwriting department. Most days my mind would wander. I started taking ephedrine, which some friend had told me about, and was basically speed. It helped. I started doing the work of three people. The ephedrine helped my mind not wander onto the other things I really wanted to do. It also led to my not eating. I must have weighed 105 pounds back then. It was ridiculous. Pretty soon, I moved on to cocaine. I tried it once or twice and liked it. I could get a lot done and didn't care so much that the work was meaningless. I thought I was fitting in to the status quo better. I followed rules better. I felt happier.

As you can imagine, this only led to more problems. I did eventually stop because I began to hate the crash. It made me feel like I wanted more and more and more. All this in an attempt to be happy with my job and my life. Looking back, it was utterly pathetic. The problem was not just that I was forcing myself to do what I hated; it was that I was completely unaware that there were any other options. I didn't know what an entrepreneur was. I hadn't even imagined starting my own business. If someone had recommended this to me at age 21, I would never have thought I could pull it off, in a million years.

I still feel a little like an outlaw because I run several businesses from home while my team members live across the country, working from their own home offices. I've grown used to not being like everyone else, and it feels good. Not everyone was meant to live life according to the status quo. The economy has forced many of us to start living this way. Some are shifting by choice, and others not.

This is the new economy. Creating your own work requires an entirely different set of rules. Some of you may feel they are drastically different. One of the best ways to begin adapting to this shift is by reading the classic book *Think and Grow Rich* by Napoleon Hill. It's over a hundred years old but will help you start accepting this new way of thinking. It's not that the ideas are new, but the concepts have never really been taught in mainstream education, so the theories will feel fresh.

These changes are going to redefine the status quo. It won't mean a white picket fence, a nine-to-five job with medical insurance, and two weeks' vacation. There is a trend being shaped and it involves writing our own rules our own schedules. It doesn't disdain creativity; it thrives on it. It doesn't avoid change; it requires it. People who like change and have ideas are the ones in charge now. The outlaws are making things happen. Stability has always been an illusion. The new economy requires a different kind of loyalty: being loyal and staying true to **you**.

This means staying true to your own desires, your own lifestyle choices, and your own ideas about what makes sense to you.

It's about doing what feels good to you and living a life of truth, instead of putting yourself into a box that stifles your energy. It's about learning the skills they didn't teach us in school – the kinds of skills that build million-dollar businesses. It's about leaving the kind of legacy you want.

Rules Are for School – Know What They Are So You Can Break Them

I've always been allergic to rules. I find them stuffy and confining – shackles I'm just itching to remove. Maybe my Catholic grade school education with its many rules gave me a metaphorical rash. It could also be that my early years were cluttered with too many unhappy, stodgy, and stagnant people. I'm an Aquarius. Many of us don't like the status quo to begin with. Thinking outside the box was my game and it came natural. I'd do just about anything, if it meant freedom and space. I just never could drink the Kool-Aid. Independence is too high a priority. So I got really good at figuring out how to play the game and **win**... my way.

After coaching and mentoring others in marketing and online business, I have discovered my thinking and strategies are actually refreshing and useful. Here is a list of traditional business rules I've broken, with great results. Ready? Let's hit it:

RULE TO BREAK #1: YOU NEED A BUSINESS PLAN

I don't understand the point of a business plan. All you need is a business model that works. A business plan is just a waste of time in the beginning. I say just get started. Go make a sale, and then we're going somewhere, with something to talk about. You learn more about your business, your customers, and the potential of an idea when you get busy. A business plan reminds me of the Elvis song: "A little less conversation, a little more action please." I don't respect it. I have a *just do it* mentality and I swim best when the threat of drowning is looming. Honestly, I think most people do, they just don't give themselves a chance to consider it. I believe in testing, tracking, and tweaking as you go, having some basic objectives, and setting quarterly goals.

When you're making money, have a marketing plan that works and an organized team you can delegate to, and are seeing consistent growth, *then* you can sit down and put a business plan together. You'll likely find it's a waste of time though. You'll have more important things to do, like managing your business and your money.

RULE TO BREAK #2: DON'T WORK FOR FREE

I hear this one a lot. It's misleading, and breaking it can be the quickest way to profits. Sound like an incongruency? Listen: You're going to need testimonials and you're going to need to be able to prove yourself. You're going to need feedback in order to learn how you measure up, how to get better, and where you stand. If you have an idea you want to test out, your fastest path to cash is to offer it up in exchange for feedback and a testimonial. This doesn't mean you need to work for nothing for a year – the faster you get a service or a handful of *pro bonos* done for someone, the faster you will get paying clients.

RULE TO BREAK #3: GET AN MBA

This one makes me laugh. It's not that I don't agree that education is important, but why waste the time and money? I just don't get it. Didn't Walt Disney, Steve Jobs, and Mark Zuckerberg prove anything about this theory? If you want to be a successful entrepreneur, an MBA is not going to make it happen. I've heard over and over from my clients with MBAs just how useless they feel their education was, and how irrelevant to their success. It's baffling, really, that so many people waste their time and put themselves in debt to earn an MBA. I have highly educated friends who can't find jobs, and think going back to school to get another degree is the answer. It's preposterous. Of course, I've also had acquaintances with no degree at all struggle in business. It's not about the degree or lack thereof; it's about how you play the game, who you learn from, and what you are bold enough to implement. Learning as you go is the most powerful form of education because it's been proven to "stick" – we simply learn faster and retain better by doing.

RULE TO BREAK #4: DON'T BECOME FRIENDS WITH CLIENTS

I'm not sure how this ever became a rule of thumb, but it's not how I've played the business game. Some of my business clients have become amazing friends to whom I refer business, and I consider their friendship valuable in more ways than could ever be counted. I would agree that you will need to keep a watchful eye on that overly needy client who takes advantage and oversteps boundaries. Those types of people can suck the life out of you if you let them. Let's be honest – these people are everywhere and using common sense with them is just part of the game. It's a mistake, however, to think that friendship and relationships with other people are not part of the game too.

RULE TO BREAK #5: DON'T QUIT YOUR DAY JOB

I would never recommend someone quit their job before they are producing income in their business; however that's exactly what I did. It was this "burn the ships" strategy that moved me forward faster. If I'd had to work all day at a job I did not like and work on my startup at night or juggle the both of them, I may not have made things happen as fast. I've witnessed too many people use their job as an excuse to not take risks, or the comfort of its paycheck to keep them shackled to it.

Your Assets Come With Liabilities

I t has been called A.D.D. Maybe it's just a restless spirit and a taste for action. Whatever it is, it comes with a few drawbacks. I've come to realize I need accountability so that I don't end up baking a pie, making jewelry, and signing up for horseback riding lessons all by noon, when all I had on my agenda was to grab a coffee at Starbucks and make three sales calls.

Coaching women to make money in their businesses, I've observed that there are three distinct personality types that do well in business, and I love the challenge of helping them get to the point where they are making money each and every month.

Three Personality Types and Their Assets and Liabilities

While working with entrepreneurs and their businesses, I've had to get to know their personalities in order to help them get their business income to the level they want. I came up with the below list of personality types because it helps me help them faster. One thing I've learned while growing my coaching business, The Moxie Entrepreneur, is that we can lead people to success with strategy and steps, and tell them precisely what to do, but they will often come up against inner obstacles that will prevent them from moving forward. Helping them understand that they create their own obstacles gets them there faster. I've had to develop systems easy and exact enough for every personality type to implement.

THE DREAMER

Assets: The dreamer has no problem coming up with ideas, and thinks bigger than most. She lives in a "dream world" and has been told this most of her life. She loves to share her ideas, and is sometimes grandiose. Dreamers are "thinkers" and see things in their heads that others can't. They have a knack for spotting trends and often have a hard time living in the present moment because the future seems so much brighter. They spend a lot of time in this place in their minds – dwelling on visions and daydreams – because it makes them happier and it's exciting. Dreamers' lives are sometimes eclectic and they find repetition mundane. They are social people who love to share and listen to the ideas of others so that they can add input and vision to the conversation. The Dreamer lives so much in the future that she seems to be at least one step ahead of everyone else in her thinking.

Liabilities: The struggle for this personality type is getting started. Dreamers can't seem to get out of their heads and put one foot in front of another long enough to make their ideas come to life. They let fear prevent them from taking too much action and their many ideas trip them up. They can't stay on one path long enough to get any real traction and instead seek to share their many ideas with others. They've previously made the mistake of telling too many people what they are going to do, which later embarrassed them when they didn't follow through, and have a growing lack of confidence in themselves because of it. They love to live in their fantasies, but have no idea how to turn them into reality. Not being detailed-oriented people, they can't see the smaller steps they need to take in order to get going, and when they do begin they get sidetracked by other ideas that take them down completely different paths altogether. They procrastinate, ruminate, and stew over their ideas. They love the feeling the ideas give them. Often the Dreamer is accused of self-sabotaging behavior. They are usually trapped in a job or career they don't really like but won't ever quit because it's comfortable and they don't really believe their ideas have enough merit, so they don't bother taking too much action.

THE CREATOR

Assets: These people love to take ideas to the next step. They are the builders of the world. They love the tangible and can take an idea to the next step faster and more easily than most. They don't let fear stop them from much. They have many hobbies. They are artists, crafters, tinkerers, and constructors. They work best with their hands and are comfortable taking on a lot more than most people. They thrive in environments that let them "dig in" and can work for hours upon hours doing what they love. They create in their dreams at night. They can see the big picture but they really shine when they are in the present moment because that's where the action is. They want to move around, and use their bodies as much as their brains. They are visually and aesthetically brilliant. They are the people who will take the first, second, and third steps while the dreamer is still thinking about it. They don't need a plan to get started because the plan is in the action. They have many projects going at once, think classrooms are boring, and don't want to waste their time discussing ideas; they just want to jump in. *Why not?* is their motto. They are free spirited and love a challenge. They wonder why everyone is just sitting around. If they sit too long, their brains go to sleep. They get bored easily, and need to get things off of the ground and move forward. Not much can stop them from finding things to do. These people are bold thinkers, and are not afraid of failure. They see failure as part of the picture and find satisfaction in the adventure. They are confident in their endeavors, free spirited, and people love them. They can get in the zone best when they're given free rein to do what they love; if there are too many prescribed steps and rules, they will likely lose interest.

Liabilities: Creators detest monotony and crave change, action, and speed of implementation. When a project gets a little tricky or mundane they will move on to the next project, leaving unfinished business and wasted effort behind them. All the projects they have going at once can cause problems in their social life, and they run from any pressure to conform. They have a hard time with consistency, dashing off to start another project before the first is complete or successful. This leads to money problems; their finances are a disaster – at best they have unpaid bills constantly piling up. They think rules are boring so they rebel when they start to feel boxed in. They can't sit still, and get antsy when they are forced to. They are messy and unorganized, and struggle to keep track of their projects. When they become unsure of what to do in order to finish a project or task, they jump to the next. Other people's projects are a constant source of distraction because they want to jump in to those as well.

Unleash Your Moxie

THE IMPLEMENTRESS

Assets: These people get the most done. They are detailed and thorough, and will implement anything that makes sense. They take direction very well and are great listeners. They observe others, take note, and admire perfection. Their consistency, follow-through, and reliability inspire admiration. They make good business people. They don't mind routine and will stick with a task until it's finished. Implementresses love results and feeling productive. They are good with money, usually clean, always organized, and rarely late. These people are constant, steadfast, and level-headed. They are often comfortable with things as they are. They take things slow and think rushing is sloppy. They don't understand the need for speed; thoroughness is the most important thing to them.

Liabilities: Their need for order and simplicity means they are not the most creative of the personality types. They don't come up with ideas of their own very often. They don't necessarily dream big, and thus don't become as successful as they might be. They aren't the most forward-thinking and don't catch on to trends. They are slower than the other personality types, and live in the present or the past. When they get stuck with an idea they're implementing, they generally decide to start over or go back to doing what was working in the beginning. They aren't big fans of taking risks, and this stunts their growth. They can seem boring to others because they're focused on what needs to get done. They are the tortoise in the race. They are logical and detail-oriented, and are the most likely of the personality types to be able to make things happen with an idea – the problem is they don't always trust that the idea has merit. They don't get too excited, keep quiet about their dreams, and won't take a risk on anything less than a sure thing. They aren't the best with change – if something is working well enough, why change direction? They fear failure and looking foolish, which prevents them from stepping out and marketing what they have to offer. They can stagnate and are reluctant to get started without a plan in place.

Resistance: the Inner Bitch

Resistance is a bitch. She's ruthless. She's laughing at you, enjoying getting between you and what you want. More than anything, she relishes keeping you in your place. But I have news that can change everything for you if you listen up: It's all an illusion.

The difference between Moxie (who cranks out success on a conveyor belt) and the girl who lives and breathes procrastination and excuses is that Moxie knows that doing the work is **not** the hardest part.

It's the getting started.

That's the secret sauce: just starting.

It's putting your fingers to the keyboard, showing up at the gym, running the first mile, taking the first leap, launching the start-up. What, you thought there was more? You think there's an easier answer? There's not.

The thing to remember about Resistance is that she's a bully. Bullies go away when you take a stand, when you stand your ground. Do something a little crazy. Become adamant about getting what you want. Show her you'll do anything to get it, that you'll do the work.

From courage comes belief. The bully will believe you. Just do it. Say it. Stand up for your truth and what you want. Take action. Just start. Bust through her invisible field.

As simple as it sounds, I have to admit that Resistance is harder to beat than anything else. Did you know that Hitler wanted to be an artist? He went to Italy and applied to the Academy of Fine Arts, and later to the School of Architecture. Here's how I see it: Resistance (the bitch) kicked his ass. He lost to the blank canvas. Starting World War II was easier than getting started with what he loved doing. Staring at a blank canvas can be absolutely paralyzing. We want it so bad... but we can do the most bizarre things trying to avoid it.

I have a good friend and joint venture partner. For the past two years, she has gone at her business, searching for that one million dollar trick. This get-rich-quick approach will never work. There are no short cuts. Watching her was exhausting until I realized what was really happening. A lot of times this approach turns people into really good liars. She lies to everyone around her – even herself. She's convinced herself that the answer will come overnight in the form of some sensational idea. Not a plan, but a *trick* – a simple tactic that will make her online business explode. She's not a deceptive person. She's got an honest business and I respect her knowledge. However, she's hoodwinked herself into letting Resistance win, daydreaming about magical money tricks instead of putting in the hard work.

She'll call me up and tell me she's found the answer – a new way of getting a ton of leads or a quick $97 WordPress plug-in that will get her exposure to a million people, each of whom will buy a $1.00 item. Get where this is going? It won't ever work. These people spend most of their time avoiding the work and trying to find the easy way out. It's sad. It feels like watching a mouse in a maze without an exit. They can't see that they are wearing themselves out in an attempt to avoid confronting Resistance. Buying lottery tickets, gambling, chasing tactics, and not doing the work are all ways of letting the inner bitch win. Resistance is behind them all, and she's laughing at you.

All my friend has to do to succeed is start chipping away at the work. I was eventually forced to distance myself from her. She was more talk than walk, and she would go on and on for hours if I let her. She'd get lost in her own ideas and talk about her dreams, her rich-girl-overnight-success fantasies. She was going to take me with her on the ride if I let her. Moxie doesn't need teammates, and she's vigilant of the people around her. Even those with good intentions have to be left behind on the journey sometimes.

Resistance will eat you alive and leave you at age 80 with nothing but daydreams, unfulfilled promises, and a gigantic heap of regrets. The truth is the more we want something – the more we feel a "calling" and the bigger it feels – the bigger Resistance gets. Resistance is a nasty bitch, a bully who grows as big as your calling and as vicious as your hunger.

Just knowing this and taking this fact into account is a start. If you let it, this knowledge can put an end to mediocrity and pointless struggle in your life. Here's an important truth about Resistance: the bitch lies within. Yup, she's in you and you're feeding her. Your subconscious has created her and keeps her fed.

Don't blame your subconscious mind, though; she's not the enemy. The subconscious takes orders. That's all she does. She's been given orders from Day One. She's turning your excuses, denial, delays, sob stories, lies, and victim tales into reality. You're working your subconscious mind overtime and paying the wages to Resistance. Day in and day out, she's getting paid and you're getting swindled.

Here's an even more interesting fact: The more we fear the bitch, the more power she gets. We do that too – we give her more power. Most of us have given her the keys to the kingdom without being fully aware of what we've done.

We fed her so well in our twenties that she's able to skip meals and keep going full swing into our thirties and forties. We didn't just feed her with lies and bizarre creative ways of procrastination – some of us fed her with shopping, TV, gossip, trashy novels, apple martinis, chocolate cake, and cigarettes. Sometimes we even chose lackluster sex, hoping for enough immediate gratification to keep us from facing what we really want: that dream that will come true someday... but not today, because we just can't get started. We jam on Facebook and play around on Pinterest. We lollygag on Instagram and poke around in people's pictures, even though we don't really care about the pictures at all. We're just keeping the bitch fed. Procrastinating.

If you want to see Resistance in her full glory, look no further than the seven deadly sins.

1. Greed: Wanting too much of something
2. Gluttony: Similar to greed, but gluttony is the action of taking too much of something in
3. Lust: The need to fulfill unspiritual desires (not just sexual desires, but this is usually what lust is associated with)
4. Envy: Jealousy; wanting to have what someone else has
5. Sloth: Being too slow or lazy at doing something
6. Wrath: Vindictive anger
7. Pride: Being too self-satisfied

The seven deadly sins are all about chasing immediate gratification instead of working for things in the right time. Immediate gratification kills our dreams and feeds the bitch within. Moxie knows this and wakes up and takes over. Moxie takes notice of what the conscious mind is saying to the subconscious. She takes the reins of this self-talk. Moxie Talk is a choice. Moxie Talk is the opposite of jive talk. Moxie speaks truth. No excuses, no lies, no BS, and no victim talk.

Moxie knows it's all in the doing – in getting started and beating the bitch within. Moxie ignores people who wallow in drama. She doesn't let their BS get to her. She knows Resistance is eating at them from within, and she also knows that if they see her winning her own battle, they might just rise up and fight back too. Her awareness keeps her strong. She's ready for the battle. Sometimes battles come from people you know and love. They show up with accusations, trying to make you feel guilty, self-absorbed, greedy, or silly. Moxie is ready for battle, whatever form it comes in. She will win. She knows they do it because the more she gets a handle on her Resistance, the more they resent their own. They will eventually lose interest and find other ways to feed their inner bitch.

So what is Moxie's armor? It's work. She just does the work that needs to be done, and that shields her from it all.

Moxie is no prima donna. She works and she loves it. She gets paid for it. She knows that just getting started will weaken the inner bitch and soon it won't even feel like work. She's done it enough to know. She gets busy.

If you've ever taken up running or started a weight training program you'll remember that the first mile is the worst. Just starting is the hardest part. The first mile sucks and even the second feels like a bitch. It's that first mile or first week of training where Resistance is really raging. She's biting at your heels and causing all kinds of thoughts to come up – thoughts of quitting or failure. Resistance sees you starting to fight back, and knows her days in the driver's seat are numbered. So she brings out the big guns and wages war. Just like writing a book or blogging or marketing, business takes showing up and pushing right through the resistance and overpowering the inner bitch.

Moxie understands that small steps lead to big growth. She knows that this can happen fast, but still delays instant gratification. She thinks big, but she completes her goals in manageable chunks.

If I don't take my clients' big goals and break them down into bite-sized pieces, I know they will choke. They'll bomb. Give up and throw in the towel. Anyone would. When they go from employee to creator to innovator, they've got a lot of work to do on the inside so they can get to the work they need to do on the outside. To deal with the inside, we break down big goals into mini goals to hush up the inner bitch that wants a paycheck right away when the work hasn't been done yet.

It's amazing how often I have to lead my new clients back to the drawing board and remind them that they haven't really done the work yet. They think the results should appear before they've put in the hours. We've all done it. Especially me. We start to piss and moan and lie to ourselves about having done the work. We don't track what we've really done or watched our time, or we ignore the parts of the process we didn't want to complete. We try to blame other people. "It can't really be this hard," we say. "This isn't fair!" All lies. It's actually not the work that is too hard. It's our inner self playing small, afraid to be Moxie, take responsibility, and dig in and do the time.

In *The Slight Edge*, Jeff Olson uses the water hyacinth as an example of fast reproduction. The water hyacinth can spend 29 days putting out unseen runners to take over a pond. You may not see the outcome at first. There's no instant gratification. It can be tough to keep working with no immediate reward if you're not used to it. Much like the water hyacinth, 90% of your growth may happen overnight on the 29th day. It's outrageous, and the sensation of working without getting anywhere can leave you feeling frustrated ...unless you know the truth. Moxie knows inspiration doesn't come; it's provoked. She doesn't force it; she leads it. She begins to see that action is almost mystical. The Moxie Muse is awakened and coaxed and takes over. She is called and seduced by action.

Don't Dig for Gold in a Man's Pocket

(The Goldmine Lies within You)

"Don't marry for money, you can borrow it cheaper."

Lois Frankel

Too many women fail to see the goldmines within themselves. They focus their attention on the man with the car or the property. I understand the appeal, because there isn't anything more unattractive than a man without drive and ambition. A man who sits and watches too much TV or has no real life goal will turn me off faster than you can say "loser."

I'm talking about the women who fail to see their own capabilities, talents, or skills. Those women are putting their energy, time, and trust in men, expecting them to create a financial future for them. This mistake has led to too many women finding themselves broke, bitter, and left with nothing.

According to Kim Kiyosaki of Rich Woman, 47% of women over the age of 50 are single. 50% of marriages end in divorce, and in the first year after divorce a woman's standard of living drops an average of 73%. Of the elderly living in poverty, 3 out of 4 are women, and 80% of them were not poor when their husbands were alive. Shockingly, 7 out of 10 women will live in poverty at some time.

This isn't just because women don't know how to manage money – it's because they never believed in themselves enough to make the money in the first place. Putting energy into your own skills, talents, and dreams will pay off in the end, trust me.

Ladies, you are your own best investment. You are perfectly capable of making decisions about your future and your children's future. I learned this lesson early enough to do something about it and turned my story around fast. It took effort and focus and mentors, but I did it.

*"You are taking control of your money
because doing so will make you feel happier
and smarter, more confident, more content,
and more useful."*

Jean Chatzky

Interestingly enough, it's almost always the single mom who hits her goals the fastest because she's got kids to feed. There's nothing like that to set a fire under your ass and get you moving. I should know; I've got three of them watching me every day and depending on me to pay their bills today and college tuition later. I don't take my business lightly and it's never been a hobby. I love it but it's not a plaything to me. I'm a woman on a mission.

Most women think of their businesses as expensive hobbies. If you've got the passion to create a hobby, why not make money doing it? It just makes sense. Life is getting more expensive and the value of a dollar is shrinking. It's time to get serious about the future.

I hear a lot of people say, "I'm not into making a lot of money," or "I don't want to have money be my focus." Often those same people are struggling in their finances and doing without unnecessarily. They're doing it out of fear; the talk about not needing or wanting to make money is just a cover for their fear of rejection and other internal junk.

Here's where I'm going with this: Every day we see poverty, in this country and across the globe. Poverty is a mindset, and education can change it. I believe the battle to end poverty in our world actually starts within, one person at a time. If more of us make it our own personal mission to change the way we think about poverty, change our mindsets, and get Moxie, we change the world.

It may seem irrational to think that we can change the world, but what's really irrational is to think our actions don't create movements and ripples of change. And it's truly the way we think that spurs us into action.

Those people who talk about not needing to make money are actually doing the world a disservice. We need to make money in order to save the planet. Everything takes money. Just look around: Without innovation and growth, we die. We need money. Period. The idea that money is not important is one of the most ridiculous ideas we teach our children and it makes it impossible for them to be an asset to society. We are actually causing more suffering in the world by not teaching them to thrive. If this somehow bothers you and stirs up an uncomfortable feeling, then it's something you really need to take a look at within yourself. You've likely not made a great deal of money in your life and you need to begin asking yourself, "Why not?"

Fly Below the Radar

W omen have less ego than men when it comes to investments, money, and business. I've seen it over and over: Women are willing to ask questions, and that makes all the difference. They have fears that sometimes hold them back, but the truth is they have less ego, and that in itself is power.

Women tend to be more practical than men, believe it or not. Mike Hamilton of the Global Investment Institute writes:

> Being involved with a company that trains people how to actively trade in the stock market I have seen thousands of both men and women start off down the road to prosperity through various types of investing. Approximately 80 percent of our clients are male. But I'd wager that 80 percent of the most successful investors are women.
>
> Based on this experience, I began to wonder why it is that women tend to be better investors than men. I thought about it over and over and could not ignore the facts. Women make more successful investors than men.
>
> But why? I think it comes down to three simple words: EGO, EGO, EGO. The one thing that most men have in common is a macho ego.
>
> Men tend to let their egos make their decisions for them. They hold when they should sell. They buy-in for fear of missing out on that one big opportunity. They refuse to ask questions or to ask for help in fear of looking silly.
>
> In other words men are more interested in looking strong, knowledgeable, or successful. They invest not to get the best deal out of the market but invest so that they look good (or not look bad).
>
> Women on the other hand, are much more likely to ask questions until they fully understand what they are learning, and they are usually more interested in the goal, (in this case making money) than they are in impressing the people around them.
>
> Usually when people think of investing, they think of taking chances and risks, but the truth is that investing has much more to do with emotional intelligence than most people

realize. Emotional intelligence is the ability to think objectively about a situation and not get too emotionally involved in it. Women, in general possess a high emotional intelligence.

This quality makes women great investors. Rather than investing according to what will make them look good, women will invest according to a plan – not according to what mood they are in or whether they will be "right" or "wrong."

Shying away from asking questions for fear of looking stupid is really stupid, and people who do it don't get any smarter. Some of the smartest women around are the ones who come up to me and begin asking questions after I give a talk to a group. The gals who avoid asking me how I do what I do online are the gals who struggle. Their egos are getting in the way of their growth.

Asking for help works. Smart girls know this. Competitive as I am, I have had to learn that it doesn't pay to attempt to look smarter than I am. In fact, it's a sure road to failure.

I learned early on in elementary school that asking for help from a teacher who was willing to give it was always the fastest path to success. It just makes life easier. Before the age of GPS navigation systems, I always stopped to ask for directions while driving, because I noticed it always saved a ton of time. I always asked for short cuts too. I've never met a woman who was unable to ask for directions in a car, but most men I've known won't. They'd rather drive around in circles with their egos intact than pull over, ask a simple question, and get there on time.

I believe that investment groups, business groups, and online learning groups are more likely to draw women for the same reasons. Men tend to want to avoid looking like they don't know what they are doing or appear weak by asking questions. Ladies, use this to your advantage. Asking questions is like asking for the keys to the kingdom. Eventually you'll get them handed to you if you ask good questions.

Low self-esteem and low self-worth are linked to not asking questions too – it's all about ego. But there is a real advantage to flying below the radar and not letting your ego get in the way.

Dolly Parton said that early in her career, men often didn't see beneath the over-the-top country persona she created to drive her success: "Well, I certainly got hit on a lot and a lot of men thought I was as silly as I looked. This worked to my advantage. I look like a woman but think like a man, and in this world of business that has helped me a lot. By the time they think that I don't know what's going on, I done got the money and gone."

Begin asking questions, even of yourself. Ask yourself, "How am I creating this?" or "How am I attracting this?" Things will begin to shift. The answers will come, and you'll begin to see connections with everything and everyone you come in contact with. You'll start loving more and seeing the possibilities. Your compassion will grow, and your curiosity will begin to guide you like a compass. You'll start to really feel the power of your emotions, and begin to see that your emotions are actually telling you much more than you ever imagined. Taking responsibility for everything around you will actually compel you to change.

Jealousy: the Weed in Your Garden

*"Envy comes from people's ignorance of, or
lack of belief in, their own gifts."*

Jean Vanier

When someone has what we want or seems to be having all the luck, we tend to feel jealous. This is natural, but it's also a sign that you're stuck on the verge of something and you need to switch up your thinking.

For instance, you may feel envy when your friend decides to start a business, throws up her website in a matter of days, starts posting great headshots of her recent photo-shoot on Facebook, makes bank, hits a money goal of hers, moves to Florida, and buys a boat. This may bring up a whole host of crappy feelings about yourself if it's something you've always wanted to do, or if you are stuck in an unhappy place in your life.

You may feel like she doesn't deserve it, because *you* were the one who made honor roll in junior high while she was always taking easy classes and being the class clown. You may be infuriated at the injustice. You may wince at the outcome. You may make up excuses about why you haven't been able to do what she's doing. You may find yourself saying things like, "She never was very responsible," or "Well, she isn't married so she can do whatever she wants," or "She's just always been lucky and gets all the breaks." You may find yourself giving her backhanded compliments or stirring up conversations about her dirty past or steering her toward gossip to keep her down on your level.

A better way to deal with your jealousy is to get excited about the possibilities for yourself. You've got to start pulling those weeds out of that crap garden you've grown. Those damaging thoughts are signs that you're in the perfect place to start working on your Moxie and turn it all around. If you find that you want those things and experiences that she's been bringing into her life, just spin that crappy thinking to help you put the odds in your favor and get the same outcome. The truth is she's got Moxie and you don't... yet. It doesn't mean you can't acquire all that she's acquired; there are a million different ways to get exactly what she has, if you just emulate her Moxie mindset and decide to get over yourself.

Talking smack about her and her past is a sign that you're feeling pretty awful about yourself. It's also a pretty good indication that you've been feeling stuck, unhappy, fixed, frozen, and glued to misery in a lot of areas of your life. You may feel stuck in a job you don't like or you may even feel stuck in a marriage that feels dead to you. Resentment, blaming, and all of the negative junk that goes with it is likely attracting a whole host of people, circumstances, and experiences that you don't want – but you haven't taken the time to work on the inner stuff and get it cleaned out, so you feel helpless. Those weeds have been growing out of control and you can't even see what you want anymore. They've overgrown and overtaken the dream you once had.

The truth is that you're the one attracting all of it. Every single irritating, unfortunate, and painful circumstance is being attracted to you because your limiting thoughts have turned into a crap magnet. Have you noticed yourself complaining? Have you noticed that what comes out of your mouth is only a small fraction of what goes on in your head? Remember this: *Every complaint is an affirmation that you want more of it.*

I see it all the time. One of the things I help women with when they are starting out or feeling stuck in their businesses, is to find their own inner Saboteurs. We go in, analyze their beliefs about money, and begin cleaning out the shoddy, useless stuff that's causing them to feel helpless. That feeling of helplessness is a literal money deterrent. We work on their Moxie mindset because the best way to start cleaning out old useless beliefs is to find where the crap garden started growing in the first place. Pulling old weeds can be tough work because they have deep roots. Finding out where the roots are and pulling them up and out is the only way to get rid of them for good. Pulling these weeds out for good can change a person's money circumstances practically overnight.

Not only does it feel good to realize there are solutions, but it's refreshing and empowering to know that your circumstances can turn on a dime – it's all a matter of putting a plan together to go with your newfound Moxie mindset.

Taking back your inner Moxie, breaking old habits, and deciding to take actions that actually serve you and bring about the results you desire can be amazing and transformational in all areas of your life. Your relationships with people will change. Your outlook will get rosier. You will want to experience more of life. Some have even told me it frees them from depression, and that they've actually stopped taking antidepressants. It's a total inner Moxie Makeover.

Women in my Moxie U program have begun to attract amazing circumstances and people – really cool coincidences – that feel like miracles. Truth is, everything is interconnected and when we begin to see everything as working together to fulfill our desires, we are finally seeing the big picture. And that's when things really start happening. That's when **life** starts happening.

Moxie & Me

Hurting People Hurt Others

Growing up, my mother called me a quitter. I wanted to play the saxophone as a child, and she told me that it wasn't worth her spending the money on it because I wouldn't stick with it. Truth be told, I did quit many things when they got tough. She saw me struggle in math or start a project only to turn around and quit. But the bigger quitter was her. My mother gave up on me, and in fact rarely even had the faith in herself to do much of anything other than gossip and create drama.

It took me years to understand the concept I'm about to share with you: Hurting people hurt others. What she spoke to me was what she felt about herself. This lesson is one we all need to hear to fully understand: What we say to others is usually what we feel about ourselves. What bothers us about others is what we see in ourselves and want to change.

My mother also called me a fighter. Not to my face, but she'd tell the story of how I fought to live right after I was born. I always loved that story. Apparently I was given little chance of survival after my birth due to internal bleeding. It came on suddenly and without explanation, and the doctor felt it was best to tell my parents that I could very well not make it through the night, and to seriously consider making arrangements in case I didn't. Part of these arrangements included having a priest read me my last rites. So the joke was that when the priest read me my last rites I decided, "I'll show them! They aren't going to tell me what to do!" And I fought it and won. I suppose it's true, because I lived through the night and have had next to no medical issues since then. In fact, I'm healthy as a horse. But when my mother would tell that story she'd always mention that I have always been a fighter. I took that seriously. Maybe it was a self-fulfilling prophecy or a role my mother thrust upon me. Whatever it was, I managed to attract fights everywhere I went. I wouldn't consider myself a bully by any means. However, bullies found me, and they always seemed to find the people around me. I would intervene in an attempt to protect them, which usually resulted in throwdowns, slapping matches, and hair-pulling fits of rage. Not pretty, but a part of my life for many of my younger years. Three suspensions in high school led to the same conversation between my mother and Mrs. Axe, the school officer: "Crystal has always been a fighter... it's in her blood." I must have believed it.

Fighting was very much a part of my home life, just like it was part of my mother's. We tend to live out the same scenarios we learned in our childhood environments, whether we liked them or not ...unless we break the chain and do the inner work to change things. My mother grew up in a home with more insults and punches than I ever did. She lived it and learned it and breathed it until she *became* it. She would have had to do a tremendous amount of inner work and healing in order to become something different. Her pain was bigger than her desire to change, though. This is the case for many people, carrying around pain that turns into self-talk – too defeating and embarrassing to repeat.

Unfortunately, for years I did not understand this, and took her words and physical abuse to heart. For years I thought I was unworthy of being treated with respect or kindness. For years my self-talk was ugly. I abused myself more than anyone else ever could. I attracted relationships with people who abused themselves too. I stayed in an abusive relationship for years, hiding the truth and believing I somehow deserved it. I tolerated being slapped, hit, shoved, and pushed around. It was what I knew, and as much as I hated it, I was comfortable with it. We all gravitate to a place of comfort even when it is miserable. If misery is what you know and your subconscious mind feels comfortable with it, you will choose it subconsciously. We will choose it in the people we surround ourselves with and that choice will, in effect, create our lives. We will stay in careers we do not like or that do not align with our passions; we will choose partners who hurt us and continue to rip away at our self-esteem; we will choose neighborhoods that do not complement our true desires or aesthetic tastes. We will go where we really don't want to go and live our lives in a way that makes us lost, miserable, and painfully unhappy. Think of your subconscious mind as a conductor and your life as the orchestra playing. Or think of your subconscious mind as a painter and your life as a canvas. If your subconscious mind is full of untruths – beliefs from your past about yourself or other people's opinions of you – that are ugly, dull, or undesirable, then the painting of your life will most certainly be ugly, dull, or undesirable.

The subconscious mind is loaded with every memory we have, and 80% of our daily actions are controlled by the subconscious mind. Just think about that scary thought for a second. You may just be painting yourself a picture of the life you don't want. You may be conducting some pretty scary and undesired music – music from the score to a Freddy Krueger movie with a bad ending, rather than the box office smash love story you truly desire.

The next time you hear about a woman living years with an abusive husband and you shake your head and roll your eyes at her stupidity for tolerating such treatment, just know that you too have done things that leave others scratching their heads and wondering why. Just like that woman, you were being controlled by your subconscious mind and have done things you truly did not want to do – things that you had no real conscious ability to stop from doing. I mean, how could you? You didn't know that you could clean out the garbage in your subconscious mind – all that's stopping you from getting what you truly want. And neither does she.

Dance to Your Own Music

"Only when I'm dancing can I feel this free."

Madonna

When I was about 6 years old, we lived in a small town in Illinois, in a community in which everybody knew each other rather well. The annual festival was usually held in the central park, and that year there was going to be an "It's a Small World After All" performance. I was invited to play the part of Little Miss Hawaii because apparently I looked Hawaiian. (I didn't think so, but my long dark hair was apparently the closest thing to a Hawaiian look in the town.) I got to wear a sarong and a flower in my hair. I was pretty excited. My part was to do a hula dance across the stage. I was psyched up about it and remember getting nervous days before. The whole town would be watching.

When the night came, I was escorted in my Hawaiian getup to crouch down in front of the stage and hide a bit so that I would be away from view and ready to jump on stage when cued. The show went on and on for what seemed like an eternity. I was crouched down, sitting on my feet in the grass. Then the moment came, and I got my cue.

Oh my God!

I tried to jump up on my feet and take the left side stairs onto the stage but my feet were completely numb. My legs were asleep and my feet felt... gone. Nothing. I couldn't much stand up, let alone walk. Mrs. Winter waved frantically to me, motioning me to get up and take the stairs. I could only stare at her. I was frozen and in shock at what was happening. One by one, people began to notice Mrs. Winter waving her arms, and soon all eyes were on me. Their stares felt like daggers piercing my body. I panicked. Time stood still. I was about to have the most humiliating experience of my 6-year-old life.

I knew I'd be in for it if I blew this and embarrassed my family. I remember thinking, *Why did they ask me to do this?* They must have thought I was something I wasn't. Something special. I couldn't do anything right, and now everyone would know. I was a fraud. Not only was my Hawaiian heritage a big fat lie, but I couldn't even fake it.

That's when I made a decision. I was **not** going to let them find out I was a fraud, unworthy of being Little Miss Hawaii. Even though I thought I was unworthy, I was committed to hiding the truth.

I jumped up and started moving my feet. I moved them as fast as I could, and hula'd myself all the way to the stage to wake them up. I didn't just hula – I jumped up and down, stomping my feet, even throwing in a few extra dance moves just to make sure my feet were awake. I could hear people in the audience laughing, and I knew that they knew it wasn't part of the show, but liked it anyway.

I learned a few things that night. I learned that I liked to make people laugh. I learned the power of faking it till you make it and not taking yourself too seriously. I learned that no matter how bad it feels inside, you can turn it all around on a dime. You just need to make a move. If they laugh, laugh with them so they don't see you sweat.

I also learned that no matter how much you're panicked inside and feel like you're about to make a complete idiot of yourself, there is always time to save face – just stand up and move forward with a Moxie attitude. You may not feel your feet, but the floor will meet them and you will not fall as long as you have the courage and faith to see it and believe it. Just take that first step, that first stomp, and throw in a quirky dance move if you have to. That will just make it more extraordinary.

As very young children, we trust ourselves more and have more faith. We instinctively know to just stand up and we don't care much what people think. Then, as we move through the years and experience more and more judgment, something creeps into our psyches. We decide we don't like people laughing at us for being different or for dancing our own little jigs.

We panic. We freeze. We lose our Moxie.

Business takes balls ...or ovaries. Either way, you've got to grow a pair. It takes doing your own dance when you can't feel your feet or the ground beneath them, knowing that the floor will come up to meet your feet or you will be given wings to fly. Either way, you've gotta make a move toward the stage.

Building a business takes courage like you've never known before. Blind faith. The stage is there and you will need to get up and dance your dance right up to those big scary lights. You just have to keep telling yourself that it will all work out. It will be okay. You won't fall – or if you do it won't be nearly as bad as your mind makes it out to be.

You may have to work a little harder. There will be times when others are sitting on the couch comforting themselves with a movie or TV while you are working late into the night. It may feel lonely or uncomfortable. You will need to use this time to get reacquainted with your internal Moxie.

You have to be willing to go deep and get to know yourself on a whole new level. You've got to be willing to put in the hours. When you do, you'll begin achieving things you've never done before, finally doing what you love, and feeling freer than you've ever felt. Commitment, dedication, and endurance will feel like a drug – the perfect elixir for your ailing soul. Your soul has a purpose, something linked to what you love to do. We were meant to be passionate, creative, spiritual beings, to go big and wide.

The Ring

*"Whatever we plant in our subconscious
mind and nourish with repetition and
emotion will one day become a reality."*

Earl Nightingale

I was 7 or maybe even 8 years old. I was sitting in the back of the big blue Buick on a crisp fall day. I remember waiting for my mother to come out of a store in the little town of Mattoon, Illinois – the town I was born in, just like everyone else in my family. I didn't think too much about what store she was in or why she was there. As she slid back into the front seat with a little bag, the energy in the air was different. She was happy about something, and that was rare for her. She announced that she had bought herself a Lindy Star ring. She was no longer going to wait for Dad to buy it for her; she had decided to buy it herself. Even at my young age I could tell she was buying it out of spite, with a smug I'll-show-him sort of air. She frequently complained about what Dad wasn't doing to show his love for her. We were always aware of just how annoyed and disappointed she was with our dad. If he bought her something for her birthday, it wasn't the right item, color, or shape. It took me years to understand my mother's internal pain and how love starved she was. As we drove off from the store that day she decided to swing by a drive-thru restaurant. She turned around to me as I was sitting in the back seat, and did something that I will never forget as long as I live. She handed me a small box, smiled, and said she had bought me a gift too. It was a little red ring box. To say I was excited would be an understatement. I will never forget that feeling. I was so surprised and delighted you could have heard me bubbling with excitement.

When I opened the tiny velvet box I sat in complete shock. My 8-year-old heart shattered and dropped right through my body, through the car floor, and down onto the cold cement ground of the drive-thru. What sat in that box was the beginning of something traumatic and devastating – a symbol of the next 30 years of my life and all its troubled relationships and painful

Unleash Your Moxie

lessons. It would determine how I perceived myself (and therefore how others perceived me.) It would cause feelings of low self-worth that would attract others with their own feelings of low self-worth, people I would allow to treat me badly. It set the stage for too many problems to count.

The box was empty. There was nothing in the box but air and the purple velvet lining. As I sat bewildered and confused, I looked up to see my mother smiling.

She laughed and said "Ha! Did you really think I bought you something?" I remember feeling worthless, stupid, and humiliated by the twisted little trick she had just played on me. I remember wanting to cry, but holding it back and forcing a fake laugh, telling her I knew she hadn't really bought me anything. I can still feel the sting of this confirmation of my worthlessness. She had proved to me what I'd already begun to learn – that I was not worth even a ring in a box. My worth consisted of an empty box, and to think anything different was a joke.

> *"Our subconscious minds have no sense of humor, play no jokes and cannot tell the difference between reality and an imagined thought or image. What we continually think about eventually will manifest in our lives."*
>
> Robert Collier

In medicine, pathology is the study of the causes of disease. In life, pathology is the disease; the stuff going on beneath the surface, passed on to you – the family patterns that you can see and feel even though no one ever talks about them. This pathology is behind much of our behavior. We either live out these family pathologies or we attempt to overcome them – to break the chain. I chose to break the chain, and the journey has been a winding road with jagged cliffs and hairpin curves. It has had me twisting, turning, thirsty, and wandering. I did not realize that on this journey I'd find my calling, get to know my spiritual side and learn to forgive on a level deeper than I'd ever thought possible.

Just like the texture of our skin or the color of our hair and eyes, our habits – our patterns of belief and behavior – are inherited from our family. These habits are difficult to break. Their roots go back sometimes for generations. When life becomes too hard or difficult, humans often fall back on our family patterns, and it takes a strong individual to break these deeply rooted beliefs, to sit up one day and say, "Something isn't right. I don't want to be like this and I don't want to hand this down to my children." Children are unable to do this. How can children know any better, or run away from the people who are feeding and clothing them?

When I was a kid I was a reader. I read books and would ride my bike to the library to get as many as I could carry on the ride back. I couldn't read enough books. Mostly, I read fiction. I loved to read, and devoured books as quickly as I could. One particular book was about a young girl about my age who was able to leave her body at night in her sleep and travel around to different places. I was fascinated by this, and remember daydreaming of doing it myself.

When I was teenager, things were becoming more and more difficult at home, with my father's alcoholism and my mother's unhappiness. I dreamed of running away – of leaving and never coming back. I dreamed of packing the few things I owned and leaving for California or some other faraway place where I couldn't be found. I dreamed of living another life in which everything was as exciting as the books and stories I'd read, and where people liked me.

My mother taught me the silent, crushing pain of feeling unwanted and unloved. Even worse than the consistent denial of love, affection, and acknowledgement was the betrayal that took place later when she ignored my abuse by another family member. When someone who is supposed to love and care for you witnesses your beatdown and doesn't do anything to stop or prevent it, that is the ultimate betrayal.

I learned to tolerate the putdowns in order to survive. I learned that if someone told you they loved you, or if you thought they were supposed to love you, it was okay for them to treat you badly. I learned that beatings with straps and wooden boards were all signs that someone loved you.

It wasn't until after I was well into my twenties that I came to understand that my mother was just plain crazy. I'm not talking *One Flew Over the Cuckoo's Nest* insanity – she carried on an apparently normal life, while holding down a job. I'm talking about emotional instability resulting in sudden, violent outbursts inside the home. I never heard it talked about as abuse or mental illness.

I took it personally. In my story, my mother's behavior was about me. About how I was wrong, stupid, and bad, and how it pissed her off. As the only daughter in the family, I was shaken, slapped, beaten, and verbally abused. I see now that she was only living out what she had learned, unable to deal with a lifetime of abuse.

A ferocious slap could come at any moment – for loading the dishwasher wrong, for giving her a look or expression she disapproved of, for walking through the house with my shoes on or using a comb or brush of hers that I hadn't realized was off limits. It could happen because I put the toilet paper roll on the dispenser incorrectly or because the bar of soap had a dent in it after I dropped it in the shower. I could get a shove or a slap for shutting the kitchen door too loudly or for opening it without permission. It could happen if she overheard me say something she didn't like to a neighbor kid or if I left the upstairs window open, if I baked a cake in her kitchen or if she thought I had been in her bedroom. I was not allowed to use anything electrical in the house – the thermostat, washer, and dryer were off limits to me. I was not allowed to touch anything of hers unless I was cleaning it. Blankets and newspapers had to be folded and put back exactly where I had found them. Everything was hers and nothing was mine. Breaking any of these rules was punished with one of her ferocious slaps across the face or head. Even in my bedroom I owned nothing. If I sewed my shirt or pants she would rip out the seams. Even playing with a toy without permission could call for a slap. I was not allowed to use play-doh in case I got it on the furniture. I had it, but I never remember playing with it; it was kept somewhere high on a shelf – untouchable and not really mine, even though I had received it as a gift from Grandma. Finger paint was off limits and my paint-by-numbers set was only something I dreamed about breaking open and playing with. My brother was allowed to play with Lite-Brite, but I was not. As a child, I interpreted her behavior as proof that I was a problem child and unworthy of owning anything – not that she was just a crazy control freak.

My mother broke a little girl's innocence, curiosity, and creative spirit into a million pieces that I did not know how to pick up. It would take years of learning to be able to heal, retrain my brain, and start picking up the pieces of my self-esteem. Cleaning out the junk that was planted in my subconscious mind took sheer willpower and determination. Luckily, I was born with a boatload of that!

If you feel as if you don't have the determination to make progress with your money problems or other saboteurs, just know that it's not all done at once. It happens by chipping away at it and taking action every day.

Homeless Teen: Recipe for Success

Failing fast is a formula for success. No matter how wrong that sounds, I've found it to be right. One of the experiences that I credit with making me resilient is being homeless as a teenager.

I was 18, and had just signed up for a fully loaded freshman year in college. I was too proud, too ashamed to ask for help. I lived in my car, and everything I owned was in there. I washed my laundry at a laundromat and took showers wherever I could – sometimes at random gas stations, other times at a friend's mother's house. I would lie, and say that a water main had broken at my apartment. I remember not wanting to be a burden, feeling that somehow I wasn't worthy of a warm bed. I remember feeling like I needed to keep it a secret so that others wouldn't discover that I was such a loser, or feel obligated to help.

I was living in my car because of a family member with a severe drinking problem. I had fled with just a few items and the clothes on my back, and I was emotionally wounded. I felt that I had no one. If my own family didn't want me around, who would?

I had a full time job at a clothing store – to this day, I'm not sure how I pulled it off for as long as I did. I remember the nights, curled up in the back of the hatchback with a philosophy textbook, cramming for an exam. I remember one day, after an exceptionally grueling day at work, I felt drained and craved an actual bed to sleep in. I had very little cash left before payday, and I was losing hope. Survival became more important than completing assignments for class. I was feeling less and less motivated to show up to classes. I had no real plan for my future, and day-to-day existence began to take precedence over any long-term plans for success.

I gave up.

I can still remember the look on the administrator's face when I walked into the office on campus and asked to withdraw from all my classes. I then walked into the campus bookstore and sold my books. I walked out of that store with $40 and used it all to check into a cheap motel.

It's amazing how a seedy motel room can seem like an extravagant night of indulgent bliss, after sleeping in a brown Datsun for a month.

It was this humbling experience that made me realize just how hitting rock bottom early can set you up for success. I chose to keep that experience with me as a reminder that no matter how bad things got while building my business, as long as I didn't have to sleep in my car it was all manageable. I learned so much from that experience, and I really am grateful for it. I learned that I can do just about anything I set my mind to. Anyone can. I learned to be grateful for less to achieve more and to not take a roof over my head for granted. But mostly I learned to hustle.

There were many days I could have chosen to just sit and feel sorry for myself. I could have given in to blaming others, which would have been a sure recipe for failure. I now understand that fear – specifically fear of failure – is what holds people back.

As an entrepreneur you will have to not care what others think. You will have to take on a failure-is-not-an-option mentality. Embrace the fact that small failures are really only setbacks and obstacles. These setbacks happen to teach you what you need to know to get you where you want to be.

Taking action creates momentum, and that will always result in success. In the few months I lived in my car, I found another job. I didn't let on that I was homeless – I just used an older address on my resume, and used a payphone as a home phone number. I used that phone to make calls. This was not the age of the convenient cell phone or internet – I used the phone book and had to really hustle. I had to sell myself in an interview as if my life depended on it. I learned how to fake it until I could make it, to fake confidence and prove myself worthy in how I communicated. This is not a desperate mindset or a beggar's mentality. Far from it. If you keep your mind focused on what you want, and know without a doubt that it's there just waiting for you to come and grab it, every rejection and every setback will be tolerable. Convince yourself that you'll get what you want, and you will. The more you accept this truth, the faster the opportunities will arrive. It's the Law. The more Moxie you become through these adversities, the better you will be able to handle success. You cannot climb Mount Everest without training ahead of time.

I ended up moving 400 miles away to start my life over when an opportunity presented itself. I hustled myself out of that town to a city with more opportunities for a fresh start, but I took the experience with me. It takes a lot for me to feel lonely. I can walk away from constricting relationships. I attribute my fearlessness and high risk tolerance to those homeless days as well. I know what it's like to hit rock bottom. I don't fear it. I know I could live through it again. Sometimes it's what we fear most that happens.

It also happens to be how we achieve success. I'm not suggesting you have to find yourself homeless to succeed – that would be ridiculous. I am, however, saying that success is linked to a failing forward attitude. Failure can be a recipe for a whole smorgasbord of opportunities. Look around and listen to those who have, or are striving for, the same level of success you want for yourself. If you listen to their stories, they will tell you that they have experienced this failing forward phenomenon too. It just happens on the way to success.

This Moxie spirit got me where I wanted to be. Moxie will get you where you want to go too. Moxie isn't given. It's earned by those who prove their resilience and steadfast purpose. Moxie is never earned by those who blame others. That's true failure. We make our lives by the choices we make. We earn our luck. Luck is Moxie and it will show up when your mindset is right.

Get moving forward and see failure not as an option, but as a setback that happens to you so you can have the opportunity to earn your Moxie stripes.

Do What Is Most Natural to You – What Makes You Want to Take the Reins

"I like someone who can take the reins, who knows what they want and is strong with me."

Leona Lewis

I believe we are all made to do something – something that speaks to us in a special way, makes us unusual, and lights us up with passion. I've always liked speed, ever since I was a kid. I remember the first time I realized that I wasn't afraid of speed the way some other people were.

It was an unusual treat to go to summer camp. I went once and loved every minute of it. It was a Catholic camp in the Ozarks of Missouri called Camp Ondessonk. You name it, it had it: archery, sailboats, cabins... even a 17-year-old black bear named Tommy, who had almost been killed after biting a child. We didn't get to pet Tommy Bear the week I was there, but we were able to talk to him and feed him. That bear got more than his share of junk food! We loved Tommy.

The camp was known for inspiring physical, mental, emotional, and spiritual growth through stewardship of nature. It offered adventurous, challenging activities. To me, it was like heaven. I have never really liked tents or roughing it or even using bathrooms without shiny porcelain and perfume bottles, but I have always loved nature. I was willing to rough it as long as I got to ride a horse – better yet, to *run* a horse, at full speed. None of this riding on a trail stuff; I wanted to *run*. Wild.

Nothing was more fun or more exhilarating. Riding a horse combined three of my favorite things: nature, freedom, and speed – a recipe for bliss. If I could ride all day, every day, I was happy.

"If passion drives you, let reason hold the reins."

Ben Franklin

One of the main events toward the end of the week was a big competition. Each group that stayed together that week took part in the competition, which was made up of several activities that were judged throughout the week. There was archery, sailing, running, swimming, and horseback riding. When I heard that each of us in our group had to compete in each category, I hated the idea. I had seen some of the other girls lose control of their horses earlier in the week, and I knew I was the only one in our group who was not intimidated by the horses.

Still, I decided that we were going to win the horse racing division. Period. I'd been able to ride several of the horses and had connected with them all. I got to know their personalities and how they responded to me, and I was able to identify the horse with the most Moxie – the one that trusted me enough to let me take the lead. Full throttle. Her name was Queen, and she was definitely Moxie.

During the week, a fellow camper had let her horse take the lead and run off wild and into the woods. She had panicked, which made the situation worse. A camp leader had jumped on a horse and took off after her, and by instinct I'd done the same. I remember running Queen as fast as I could, getting as close to the other horse as possible, yelling at the rider to take the reins and pull back, to let the horse know who was in charge.

It didn't work. She cried and screamed and very nearly fell off. I could see how traumatic it was for her. I felt bad for her but could not understand why she was letting the horse sense her fear like that. She didn't understand the power of confidence. Horses can sense this. They pick up on our energy.

I told her to not show fear, to be confident and the horse would likely calm down. She didn't much appreciate my advice. She was humiliated too. I knew she would never want to get back up on that horse for the race, so once we had brought her back to camp, I immediately went to tell her that I'd race for her and to ask her to choose a category of the competition to exchange with me. She was relieved.

At the horse stables, I asked a camp leader if I could pick my horse for Friday's race. I explained that Queen and I had bonded and that it was the best choice for our group. I could tell she was a horse lover too and told me that she would watch for me that morning and hold Queen for me.

It didn't take much to win the race that day. I did it 6 times. Each participant would go through each category of the competition. I did what I had planned all along: I stuck near the stables and ran each race for my team with Queen. I knew someone might object, so I didn't mention to anyone – especially the camp leaders – that I'd be doing this. I'd learned that asking for forgiveness worked better than asking for permission.

To avoid suspicion, I changed up my look and position in each race so that each camp leader would see me once. I exchanged ball caps with team members, pulled my hair back – even ran behind the stables and changed shorts with another girl... just in case. I would move Queen to another line and turn my hat around. I would get off Queen after each race and run and hide behind the stables to avoid getting caught.

That day I ran horses faster than I ever had, and at times I grew afraid – afraid for the other girls, some of whom were running way faster than they should have been with so little experience. But also afraid for myself. No matter how confident or fearless you are or how much you love doing something, there will be times you question yourself or think about how everything could go wrong at any time. I remember feeling like I was going to fall off – at times I was almost sure I was going to. I told myself that as long as I did the same thing each time and as long as I kept my mind on that, I wouldn't fall. I didn't fall and it was exhilarating but yes, I was afraid. Not so much that I let it take over or let Queen lose trust in me... but I felt it.

There are going to be times when you will have to fake confidence. Do it. Choose faith. Don't imagine yourself falling. Imagine yourself winning. Keep intentional – focused and strategic. Just know. Know you were meant to do this. Know you were made to finish the race.

Running that horse as fast as I could that day was one of the first times in my life I felt qualified. I knew on a cellular level that I was meant to run that horse fast. It felt good.

I'm convinced there are things we were meant to do that others aren't. Some call it talent. You may think of it as skill or passion or something that just comes natural. Usually it's a talent that you loved so much that you nurtured it and got really good at it, until it was recognized as a skill – something that others notice in you. They may say things like, "You should really think about doing that," or, "You're so good at this." Something that makes you stand out in a group.

Try to remember when you were a child, shining at something that others didn't. It may have left you stumped as to how others struggled with it, when you just took to it naturally. It may have been something you did as a hobby – something you felt like you could happily do all day long: painting, building art with junk you found, or ice skating. Something you dreamt about. Something you could do as easily as breathing air. Something that put you in that "Moxie zone." Something that thrilled you to the core, grabbed your attention and turned you on like a switch. Something that made time stand still – something that, when you were doing it, nothing else mattered.

That something is likely at least part of what you were meant to do. That's your Moxie. I may not ride horses every day but I know that I can. I know that the exhilaration of speed is something that comes naturally to me. I thrive on it. I need it every once in a while and I use it to find joy in other things.

I started with a website called FearlessAmbition.com because the name resonated with me. I picked up on something that made me feel alive – something I had that not everyone had. A fearlessness, a love of speed, of just going for it full throttle. I turned it into a business. I may not have had the best business model at first, but it was something I wanted to share with the world, so I just took that first step.

Once I recognized it, I understood that my love of speed colored everything in my life. For instance, I've had to find workout routines that include an element of speed. Spinning class will keep my attention; walking won't. Yoga is a struggle for me because it's so slow and methodical. I have done it, and I love the results, but it's just not something that I find thrilling. Running sprints is thrilling to me – jogging, not so much. I need the thrill of speed in my life. When I've ignored this, and let myself go for months without it, the results are very negative. My energy dries up, and I find myself acting out impulsively. When we suppress our own love or passion, it's like taking away sunshine and water from a growing plant; it not only fails to thrive – it eventually dies. It loses its zest; the color begins to fade from the leaves. It loses its shine, and eventually fades away and dies.

Let your passion be the sun and water that your soul needs to shine. Turn your soul back on and give it what it was meant to have. I assure you that when you deny yourself what you were meant to do, it will have dramatic negative effects in your life. You may see it in your attitude, emotions, eating habits, relationships, job choices, or judgments about other people. If you don't allow yourself the pleasures that turn your soul on, you will feel resentful, ungrateful, guilty, moody, melancholy, pessimistic, and dispirited. Basically you will feel crummy. This blue spell is your soul's way of telling you that it needs passion – whatever it is that you desire on a cellular level.

There is no honor in sacrificing what your soul needs. We women do this more than men do. For some reason we feel guilty for doing the things we love. It makes no sense, and no one else is doing it to us. We are responsible for it ourselves, but it leads to pent up resentment that we eventually wind up taking out on others, wreaking havoc on our families and teaching our children to suppress their passions. That's in no way what we really want for them! By our own example, we leave a legacy of desolation and misery. I can't think of anyone who would actually want that for their children, but that is exactly what we are doing when we deny our soul the sun and water it needs.

What's Your Money Saboteur?

*"I have a tendency to sabotage relationships
and everything else in life. Fear of success,
fear of failure, fear of being afraid. Useless,
good for nothing thoughts."*

Michael Bublé

Everyone has to face the internal Money Saboteur at some point as an adult – especially women, who tend to carry around money issues for years. We can either ignore the Saboteur and deny it exists, or we can stand up and face it head-on because it means the difference between up-leveling our lives or not. It will hold us back until we acknowledge it and decide to change it.

For me it was feeling unworthy – unworthy of keeping money. I had to deal with self-sabotaging issues surrounding money so that I could continue growing my business, and I lost several thousands of dollars because of my issues surrounding money.

I'm going to get all full disclosure here and share a dirty little secret with you. Ready? Here it is:

For years I didn't have enough self-worth to manage my money, so I didn't keep track of it. The more money I made in my business, the more I lost it or blew it. It was as if I had come to feel comfortable with the number 0 in my bank account. It was totally nuts and I'm aware of that now. I had no money in savings and when I would have a lucrative month in my business, I would find ways to blow it all. I wouldn't even think that much of it. I know people who start to get antsy if they have less than $5,000 in savings, but I was running on fumes most of the time. I'd tell myself that I could always go and make more of it next week or even tomorrow morning.

I knew I could make money. Heck, I could sell snow cones to an Eskimo and I'd proven that over the years, so that's what I'd do. I made a habit of it until it was time to take my business to the next level, and hit a bigger goal. I seemed to be hitting a wall. My business had plateaued. I knew I had to do something different because, like I've always told my clients, when you want different results you've got to do something you've never done before. But it hadn't occurred to me that I had these whopping big inner issues surrounding money.

Then all hell broke loose and things got messy in a lot of ways. This will happen when you decide to go after what you want. It's all inner stuff, and it can get out of control if you're not aware of it or you ignore it and go into denial. You may even feel like you're going nuts or having a run of serious bad luck. Worse, you may feel like giving up and think you're not cut out for starting a business or taking on the responsibility of a big project or a leadership role.

The trouble began showing up in my life as tax issues, people stealing from me, and employees slacking off on the job. I even allowed a boyfriend to steal from me little by little, adding up to a significant amount. I should know exactly what that amount is... but I don't. I had suspected it all along, and had attempted to confront him about it, but I had given away my power. I had given him access and total control over one of my accounts because I believed deep down that I was unworthy or incapable of managing my own money.

I remember one night calling him up and telling him point blank that I was missing over $5,000 and couldn't account for it, and asking if he knew about the discrepancy. His exact words were, "How would you know? You never watch your money." He followed it up with, "You spend more than you think you do, so I'm sure it's your fault." I believed him. How could I argue with someone who knew more about the account and its daily balance than I did?

The same man stole an engagement ring from me, and lied about it. I gave away my power and ignored my gut over and over. I allowed people like this to stay in my life. My insecurity was making my decisions for me.

If there is one thing that growing a successful and profitable business will reveal, it's money issues. Remember when I mentioned that we all have a thermostat setting that we feel comfortable with, and that if we pass this setting, we will shut down and begin self-sabotaging behaviors in order to get us back to a comfortable level – even if it means failing or being less than we are capable of being? This may sound shocking, but my money thermostat was set to $0. My childhood had taught me to feel unworthy of having any money at all.

For years, my mother would never allow me to have cash. I didn't get an allowance, and when I earned money, she would take the money or tell me to give it back to the person who had given it to me, saying that I had taken too much for the work I'd done. She made me feel guilty about taking money from an adult, or she'd tell me the job I'd done was half-assed. This taught me to work for nothing, and that I had no abilities worthy of recognition, let alone pay.

I remember working with my brother on a paper route for a year, never being allowed to earn half as much, even though I was waking up every morning and doing the same amount of work. I remember one day being given $40, knowing full well that it was only a fraction of what he had earned and not saying a word about it. I just accepted it. That taught me that girls got paid less for the same amount of work. I was being taught that I was unworthy of having money or earning a fair amount. I was less than.

Every Saturday morning, my job was to clean the house from top to bottom – every room and every bathroom. It would take me exactly four hours. I would time it, and made sure to wake up early enough to get it done and over with so that I wasn't working while my friends were out having fun. I didn't want to miss anything. I've never regretted having to do this now that I'm an adult, because it taught me hard work and several other things. Most importantly, it taught me that I didn't like to clean houses! My point is that I was never paid for this work until after a family therapist asked my parents why I wasn't paid an allowance. It took a family therapist with a degree in psychology to convince them that if they paid me an allowance I would likely have a better attitude about the work, thus building confidence and having an overall positive experience from it. This therapist acted as something of a referee for me. As much as I hated going to family therapy, I liked that he helped me communicate and navigate the quagmire of my family life. Before this, I never felt heard. I felt dismissed as a problem in the family and beneath everyone else. I was not worthy of their respect or even of having my feelings taken into consideration. I will come back to this point later; it's important to go back to where your first memories about money lie, and attempt to understand the story behind your feelings and the stories you made up about your childhood experiences in order to make sense of them all.

Growing up, I had very few clothes and belongings. My mother would not shop for clothes for me, and on the few occasions that my father gave me money for clothes, he made me account for every dime with receipts for the few items I'd bought, all the while telling me in great detail just how much penance he'd be paying for doing me this favor. My mother did not allow my father to do things for me. Any extra love or attention he would extend to me would cause all hell to break loose in the house. He would be emotionally punished, sometimes for weeks.

I heard about it all the time. He constantly told me how jealous my mother was of me, and how she made his life miserable. I would feel guilty and shameful for having him do me this "favor," leaving me feeling deeply unworthy.

When he went over the receipts with me, he would accuse me of keeping some of the money; this made me feel untrustworthy and irresponsible – incapable of managing money and unworthy of basic of necessities like clothing.

We kids steered clear of my mother at all costs. When she would come home from her part-time grocery clerk job, we would all scatter and hide. She was unhappy about everything. She'd start out complaining about a messy house or start accusing us of messing up her kitchen, leaving things out of place. She'd complain about how much her feet hurt or how someone at work had caused her grief. I remember hearing how certain customers had made her job more difficult, or how people with food stamps would use them for expensive lobster tail and how much it pissed her off. It would eventually escalate to a screaming match with my father if he was the only brave soul to stick around. We kids would usually hide and cover our ears. It would turn into an evening of stomping, screaming, yelling, and slamming doors, all coming from one mouth and one person: my mother.

One night right before Christmas, she had decided to get my Christmas shopping done early and let me pick out my own gifts, which I had decided were clothes. This was the first year she'd ever done this. She picked a night after working all day standing on her feet, and she immediately made it clear to me that she was exhausted and that I should feel extremely grateful to her for doing this for me. Every store I stopped in, I was ridden with guilt while she stood outside of the store, looking haggard and worn out. I felt horribly guilty. The first time I ever really remember her spending alone time with me – just the two of us shopping together – turned out to be a guilt trip from hell. It only reinforced my belief that I was a burden and didn't really deserve any of the clothes she was buying me from her hard-earned paycheck. It was a feeling I knew I never wanted to feel again.

I never realized that feeling unworthy was a problem for me until I did the inner work and had to face the truth. In order to turn my money troubles around, I had to uproot the problem by going directly to the source, to where it all started. These early memories were the deep, gnarly, negative roots of my feelings about money. I had to come to the realization that my mother's bad feelings about her life had nothing to do with me, and that she had projected her own ugly money issues onto me. Her feelings about money and her miserable life had nothing to do with me and everything to do with her lack of inner Moxie. Her feelings of being trapped, underpaid, and overworked kept her feeling like a victim. Victims are never Moxie.

After discovering the root of my feelings about money, and realizing that I felt undeserving of ever having any, I had to get real with this very disturbing problem. My carelessness and total neglect of money – the way I was throwing it away as fast as I could make it – was a reflection of my self-worth and my feelings of guilt around it. It was my feeling of unworthiness that was keeping my thermostat set at $0, and it was anything but Moxie.

You may have issues of your own about money that are holding you back, and keeping your thermostat set far below what you are capable of or should be making in your business, job, or career. The good news is that something can be done about it once you acknowledge it. The most unfortunate and devastating thing about these inner Money Saboteurs is that neglecting them makes your life miserable and stagnant. And to top it all off, we pass these struggles and beliefs on to our own children.

Fear of Failure

Fear of failure used to drive me. As a child growing up in Decatur, IL, I thought struggle and mediocrity were my only options. I lived in a trailer with my family until the age of three, and then in a lower middle class home. I swallowed phrases like "Money doesn't grow on trees" and "College isn't for you; it's for smart, rich kids." At school I barely scraped by with a C average and wore clothes other kids pointed and laughed at. I can remember my socks getting soaked through my cheap K-Mart brand tennis shoes and my dad inserting a piece of rubber he had found at his factory job to the bottom in an attempt to add a few more months of wear. As a kid I dreamt of owning a pair of Nikes, which at the time were all the rage. I was bullied in high school my freshman year for not wearing the latest fashions, and failed three classes my first semester – just another reminder that I wasn't good enough. While some kids worried about not getting an A in Biology, I worried about getting to Biology class in one piece. At 18 I dropped out of college and sold back my textbooks. Giving up and scraping by were all that I knew.

Today I not only have a college degree (the first in my family) but have excelled at sales and marketing, sold commercial real estate, started several businesses, and now run my education business MoxieU.com from home. I've lived in a log home overlooking 25 acres of tranquility in Iowa with my three children, and recently moved to Florida, near the ocean. I have customers all over the world and fly them in to spend two days with me and build their dream businesses and lives.

Everything changed for me when I decided to hire a mentor after hearing author and speaker Bryan Tracy say, "You become the five people you spend the most time with." That statement gave me a jolt down my spine because I realized that I was surrounded by people who were horribly dissatisfied with their lives and were victims of circumstances. I knew I didn't want to be either of these things. In fact, I realized most of the people I'd surrounded myself with most of my life had similar victim mentalities and chose mediocrity over Moxie.

So, against many of those same people's advice I made the bold decision to invest in a mentor. That was the best decision I've ever made and I've never looked back. Not only did I get the perspective I needed but I found the Moxie I'd always had, just waiting to escape.

My mission and passion now is inspiring others to create their own entrepreneurial ventures just like I did. Turns out anyone can bounce back when they decide to. Failing early was one of the best things that could have happened to me. Having failed so much in my early life, I realized it fueled my love of creating something out of nothing. I don't fear being homeless or living in my car because I've already done that. Once you've hit rock bottom, there's only one way to go, and that's **up**. When you apply Moxie to your actions there isn't anything that can't be achieved, and the speed at which you achieve it is only limited by the amount of Moxie you give it.

Moxie means ambition and courage. Sometimes the only way to get Moxie is to believe you can acquire it. Moxie is Faith in Action, and action only happens when you know full well what you don't want, and decide what you *do* want.

I try to live life looking fear directly in the face and laughing. Most people fear being homeless and it is a humbling experience, however once you've faced your fear you know exactly what to do to turn it around. That doesn't mean you have to hit rock bottom, but it does mean you really need to roll up your sleeves and ask yourself, "What is it that I really want, what is stopping me from getting it, and what will happen if I don't get it?" The thing that is most often stopping us from getting what we want is inaction, which is the cousin of procrastination and the sister of fear. They are all connected, and once fear is replaced with Moxie the world will reveal a path laid out for you like a yellow brick road to Home.

The more Moxie in your attitude and actions, the more success you attract into your life. When you begin to realize that everything is within your power, your every thought has magic in it, and your every wish can come true, it changes the game and you become the winner. Mediocrity and Moxie are both decisions. They both require facing fears; the only difference is that Moxie will reveal to you the hero within and Mediocrity will only reveal the victim.

The Ring of Fire

I gave birth to my son at home by choice. I had done a lot of reading about natural birth and how much better it was for the baby and mother. It just made sense to me. After learning about the epidural and what it was going to do to the baby, I came to the conclusion that it was going to be more uncomfortable for me to get the epidural than to have him naturally.

Yes, it hurt like hell and yes, I dropped the F-bomb as the baby was crowning. In fact, the first push resulted in nothing because halfway through the push I freaked out and stopped. I thought *Holy hell, what have I done?* and immediately went into I-can't-do-this mode. I panicked and ordered my midwife to call 911 to come get the baby out of me …which was laughable because a truck full of EMTs wouldn't know what to think of a woman on the floor of her bedroom, screaming at them to grab a pair of forceps. For one split second I was attempting to convince myself I couldn't do it. I wanted out. I wanted to quit. I wanted to give up. That's what we all want to do just seconds before we break through to freedom. I see it in business as well.

Except that in this story I'd burned the ships. There was no getting out of it. There was no calling 911, no giving up. My midwife said the magic words: "You've got to do this. If you push again and stop midway, the baby will keep going further back up just like it did, and you'll be pushing all night. You're fighting it instead of letting it happen." My first lesson in surrender.

That was all it took. I thought, *That hurt! There is no way I'm willing to do this all night.* So it became more comfortable to push hard and not stop than it was to push half-assed. I learned my lesson. I pushed two more times, and he was in my arms. One push for his head and one push more for the rest of him.

They call it the Ring of Fire in childbirth – that moment when you're crowning and the baby is about to appear. I call it barbaric. However, when I saw my son, I was not just amazed by this human being who had emerged from my body; I was amazed by the whole process. Any mother will tell you this. The childbirth process itself made me tough – resilient and tough. It made me Moxie.

Assessing the whole six-hour childbirth process, I have to admit it wasn't just the pushing part that changed me. Pushing took about two minutes, but the first six hours taught me focus and endurance, and reintroduced me to the whole fight or flight concept. It taught me to face fears.

It was life-changing on more levels than I even realized. I believe that childbirth is God's way of showing us what we are made of. To this day, it remains one of the most amazing experiences I've had. It gave me Moxie. I still think back to that night, and I remind myself that I am capable of just about anything.

I'd like to remind you that I still consider myself a wimp in many regards. I hate pain. I hate needles. I hate even the thought of pain. Many people who know me were surprised that I would decide to do such a thing: have a baby in my home without drugs or anything artificial to make it easy. I had made a name for myself as the pain avoider. When I decided to have the baby at home, I ensured there would be no drugs to reach for. No ambulance there in the driveway to take the pain away. It forced me to look within and just face it. No other options. No giving up. It was going to happen.

The Day My Brother Died

In 1998, I sat across from a young man, just 23 years old, as he chewed at his fingernails, lit one cigarette after another, and asked me questions about life. He was scared, uncertain, and unsure he could do what he really wanted to do. Not sure he measured up. Not sure he fit in anywhere. He mentioned his father and that he thought his alcoholism had killed his brain cells. We laughed. I tried to lighten the mood. It was intense; I could feel his depleted energy. He asked me what he should do, and mentioned that he wanted to go to school but hated the thought of it because he felt dumb and never was good at academics. The smoke in the air was a stifling cloud of uncertainty and vulnerability. I will never forget how unsettled I felt. That man was my younger brother and I loved him. That was the last conversation I had with him. He took his life just 3 weeks later. He decided to take a gun and end his life. Just like that. It broke my heart and the hearts of many others who loved him. I'll never forget that day. It felt like having my heart pulled straight out of my chest and brought me to my knees, literally.

It was April 6th, 1998. I had a feeling all that day of misalignment and grief. It was almost as if I knew of his death before I'd been told. Sometimes we know things and this knowledge rises up within us as feelings. I had one of those feelings the night he died. I was grief-stricken even before I knew he had died. I thought of him several times that day and recalled what I'd felt during our last conversation, in the room with the cigarette smoke and the unspoken pain I felt helpless to alleviate.

Things can turn on a dime. Our lives, our circumstances, and our mindsets can all change without notice. Our minds are made up of habits and beliefs we have built up through our own life experiences or adopted from others we've let persuade us. Many of us are still carrying beliefs around in our subconscious minds that were set during childhood and are quietly directing us and our actions every day.

If my brother hadn't taken his life I might not have found it within myself to change my thinking. In 1998, my way of thinking was completely different. That tragedy is still the most painful event of my life, and it caused me to search for answers. The searching not only changed my thinking, it saved my life. Many events have happened since his death, and after careful observation I can only describe them as miracles.

I'd like to introduce a way of thinking that will turn your life on a dime too, if you let it. Your life is what you have created for yourself. No one did it for you. You have decided everything and every circumstance, and it has all happened in your mind. The way you feel about people, the quirks or personality traits you tend to notice or point out about those people and how you *feel* about those people have caused you to attract more of them. When you give, you get. What you focus on expands, and I truly mean that in every sense of the word. What you focus on, what you fear, what you love, what you worry about, what you don't want, and what you do want... you will bring it about. The old saying, "What goes around comes around," has more truth than you can possibly imagine.

Without question and without a doubt, anyone who has brought a truly wonderful or desired thing into their life has brought it about by using one of the greatest powers in the world – a power we all have to use. It's our own mind coupled with our feelings:

Image + Feeling = Outcome

When we set out to start something, win something, or achieve something, we start with a feeling. That feeling is usually desire or passion, also known as love. For whatever reason, we love that thing we desire. A runner loves running and the feeling it gives him – whether he loves the euphoric feeling exercise gives him or the feeling of achievement he gets from crossing the finish line, it's the feeling that he's after. If he loves horses or horseback riding, he loves the feeling the act gives him. A guy (or a chick like me, for that matter) loves the feeling of riding a motorcycle. He may love the speed or the feeling of freedom on the road. Harley Davidson has described their target customer as "a middle aged man that typically wears a suit to the office and wants to roll into town and have people think he's a bad ass." That, my friends, is a *feeling*.

Feelings and emotions rule our world and our lives and yet we don't give the fact much thought or consideration. Ever notice that when you have feelings of anger you tend to attract angry people? When you're in a hostile mindset and are driving around ticked off, that's the day you manage to attract a guy with road rage or a woman who unexpectedly flips you the bird. Feelings of low self-esteem tend to attract others with low self-esteem also. We can say that opposites attract but it's more accurate to say that like attracts like.

It's true. If you think back to certain parts of your life you'll see a resemblance between your state of mind and the people you were surrounding yourself with. There is proof all around us. From neuroscience to nuclear physics, you'll find documented studies of energy and how the mind is part of that energy. It's not something you should ever downplay or disregard. It's real.

It's no coincidence that my uncle took his life at a very young age by the same method as my brother. Some believe that there is a genetic code within us, that we carry around similar life lessons and have a life assignment much like our parents and ancestors. Some families have a poverty mindset that is handed down from generation to generation, like alcoholism. I also believe that there are no life sentences. We have the ability to make choices and changes on a cellular level, and redirect the family legacy.

After my brother died I set out to do that. It was not necessarily conscious; I just knew I was hell-bent on figuring things out after my brother's suicide. I began learning more and more about the mind and how it works. You could almost say that I became obsessed. I was a couple of credits shy of a psychology degree, but my education didn't touch this topic like it needed to. I no longer believe that all people are destined to take anti-depressants for the rest of their lives or that they will always be drug addicts or alcoholics. I believe we can change our destinies on the cellular level by changing our thoughts, which leads to changing our actions.

I remember a fear rising up in me when I had my son. Fear that he could have a genetic predisposition to self-hatred, low self-esteem, and limiting thoughts that could lead him to harm himself like his family members had – not only on my side, but on his father's side too. My son has two uncles and a grandfather who committed suicide, and this scared me.

I believe we choose our life lessons before birth. I'm also convinced we can evolve and retrain, with work. The subconscious mind is like another self that we can connect with. We have to start by understanding our own unique subconscious mind. It's like a hard drive that's been wired with our childhood experiences and other outside influences. This hard drive is what is driving our actions every day, dictating our daily lives.

All this is not "new age." Over a hundred years ago, in the classic book, *The Science of Getting Rich*, Robert Wattles describes this phenomenon as a science. These truths are a part of this world and have been for centuries. They are actually revealed in the Bible and Jesus himself spoke of their significance. Ask, believe, and you shall receive. Sound familiar?

Listening For Answers

I spent the year after my brother died attempting to find answers. That's what I do. I love to research, and whenever I research something in my life or my clients' businesses, I always grow in some way. I find answers that stretch my life and get a little closer to my own truth.

When you have your radar up and your eyes peeled, looking for answers, you'll attract them fast – trust me. Unless, of course, you're hell-bent on keeping a small mind and a know-it-all attitude. We all have mental blocks, and these blocks keep us blind to the truth until we're Moxie enough to let the answers in. During that excruciatingly painful year after Jeff died, I was definitely attracting truth. Have you ever heard that when God or the Universe is trying to tell you something, the answers will start hitting you over the head like a two-by-four? That's what happened to me.

One night I had been out with a friend, drowning my grief at the 801 Chophouse (best food in Des Moines) and after two bottles of wine we went home. I hadn't realized just how much I'd had to drink until I was lying in bed, with the room spinning. It wasn't just spinning – it was doing pirouettes, and before I knew it my body was having convulsive fits.

A couple of weeks earlier, I'd been given a prescription for Wellbutrin and had been taking it regularly to help with the grief. While drinking on medication wasn't my brightest decision, in my defense anyone who has experienced this kind of grief, guilt, and regret can tell you that grieving people tend to care less about healthy choices and outcomes, and more about relief and numbing out. Mixing drugs and alcohol is just not the way to heal. Long story short, I ended up in the E.R. that night and learned a lesson I'll never forget.

After a long night of piercing bright lights, screams and moans from other patients, and lectures from a nurse from hell about mixing booze and prescription drugs, I woke up the next morning in a room that was just as noisy. The sounds of a man down the hall yelling for a bedpan woke me up and punctuated another voice speaking words I will never forget as long as I live.

My head was pounding and I could barely lift my head to see where this voice was coming from. The voice was saying (or bellowing) "The world we live in is the world we choose to live in, whether consciously or unconsciously. If we choose bliss, that's what we get. If we choose misery, we get that, too." He went on and on, saying things I'd never heard anyone say before. "People growing in a certain environment consistently model what they see. If you grow up in an environment of wealth and success, you can easily model possibility, wealth, success." What really got my attention was this: "You can create in your mind the experience you desire in the future... as if it were here now. Just like past experiences can change your internal representations – and thus what you believe is possible – so can your imagined experience of how you want things to be in the future. The kind and intensity of belief you have, the amount of potential you unleash, the kind of actions you take, and the kind of results you get are all linked. **We create our reality**, and it can be changed... in an instant!"

I was mesmerized. I couldn't quite sit up, but I finally did open my eyes just enough to realize that the voice was coming from the television the nurse had flipped on in my room. The man who was speaking was Anthony Robbins.

When I left the hospital that morning, I had a totally new perspective. Even though I'd just experienced a night of shame and regret and had a headache from Hades, I felt like I'd just been given the answers I'd been looking for. I felt like I'd just been given hope.

Not much came of it, though. That feeling didn't quite last. Two days later, in my own home, the same voice came crashing down on my ears, shaking me. I heard the same words from the same voice. I ran downstairs and sure enough, there he was again – Anthony Robbins, this massive man with an equally massive voice, being interviewed on The View. I immediately stopped what I was doing and took notice. How could I be getting the same message the very next day? Sure enough, the very next day after that, I heard him for a third time on the radio, and that's when I found a bookstore, pulled my car over, and bought his book. I felt like the message was personalized just for me, like God was hitting me over the head with the answers I'd been asking for. That's what it feels like when it happens – like a neon sign or a megaphone. You just have to pay attention. Unfortunately we usually don't pay attention until we've hit rock bottom.

As I sat reading Anthony Robbins' book, I couldn't help wonder why on earth I'd never heard anything like it before. It was astonishing that in my 27 years I'd never once heard anyone speak in this way, that every one of us has the power within us to do great things. It was a concept that was foreign to me. That's when I discovered the importance of asking and acting when the opportunity appears. When I took notice, turned my car around, and went to buy Anthony's book *Unlimited Power*, that was an act of Moxie.

You need to become more proactive in everything you do. We all have a default mode. This mode is unfortunately reactive instead of proactive. This is the mistake we all make: we get so comfortable with living that it sometimes takes a tragedy to jolt us out of our numbness. Truth is, I needed to act the first time I heard his voice in the hospital. We all need to start acting a little more and numbing out a little less.

It took me years to realize that my reaction to my brother's death was actually part of my talent. My curiosity, which always had me reading books, getting into trouble, and doing things I probably shouldn't have been doing when I was younger, was actually part of my gift.

I had always been ashamed that I'd had so many jobs. Society seems to celebrate years and years of loyalty at a career as some kind of proof that you can stick it out. But I had never been able to stick with a job longer than two years. This was because I was never passionate about any of them. I would either get fired (self-sabotage) or start looking for another job when I was supposed to be focused on getting raises. If this is you, don't fret it. Get over it. Seriously, ten years from now you'll be primed for success because of your many skills and experiences. The more jobs I'd had, the more experiences I had to draw on in sales and in running my own business. Those experiences gave me an array of perspectives to choose from when finally deciding on a specialty.

The Magic Baby

*"Thoughts are energy, and you can make or
break your world with your thinking."*

Joy Browne

It was just a few months after my brother died. Something about losing a loved one puts life in perspective: just how short it is and how little time we have here on Earth. It can motivate us to start really living and getting what we really want.

I had always wanted children. I love kids. I had been unsuccessful at achieving pregnancy for about four years, but I was still determined. The doctor I was working with had performed an exploratory procedure to find out if I "had the right plumbing" – these were his exact words. I did. So there wasn't really an explanation for why it wasn't working. We underwent seven artificial inseminations – two of them with Dr. Young in West Des Moines, Iowa, the world-renowned fertilization doctor responsible for the world's first set of septuplets born successfully. (I was so jealous of her. I remember thinking, *This woman gets seven kids and I get none? Not fair!*)

I wasn't ready to give up, though. I had read books about conceiving naturally. I ate the right foods, got into shape, and even became a vegetarian – drinking green juice every day that made me want to puke. I wanted this bad!

Everything I know about manifesting comes from this story, so listen up. I was hell-bent and focused and willing to try pretty much anything to make this conception happen. When you become focused, you are always led to the answers.

That's what happened to me. I was sitting in church one day when an opportunity presented itself. They needed more sign-ups in the perpetual adoration chapel in the church. It had someone praying in it 24/7. People signed up and committed to pray in shifts. There was never a moment when there was not someone in the chapel praying. I signed up.

After just a couple of weeks I noticed that there were people coming in and out behind me during my once-weekly 20-minute shift. One day I noticed there were people coming in just to write in a notebook in the back of the chapel. They would pick up the pen, write something down, and leave.

I became curious. I got nosey. I went to check out the notebook. I read page after page of touching prayer requests. I decided to write my own, and just happened to write it to Mary.

I decided to get specific about the baby I wanted. Something happened in me that day, and I wrote the words:

I need this to be easy. I am tired of trying. If there is a child I'm to adopt, show me the baby. I do not have the energy or patience to go to adoption agencies to stay on a waiting list. Just show me the baby, and I will say yes.

I decided to rip the page from the notebook and keep it. I left the chapel that day, knowing it was going to happen. I cannot explain why I felt so sure that my struggle was over. I just did.

I now know that feeling to be surrender. This was one of the few times in my life I was able to surrender. I have been a determined fighter most of my life. I had not known surrender until that day.

I pulled out that notebook paper every day. Each time I read it I had the feeling that the baby was on the way. I went so far as to buy a baby blanket. I began to prepare for it, showing the Universe (God) that I believed the baby was on the way.

I had a dream several days later. In the dream I adopted a child. She was 7 years old in the dream and I remember making her dinner. When I awoke from the dream I told my husband about it. He laughed it off. That was the only time I'd ever mentioned anything to him about adoption. I never said anything about what I'd written down on the notebook paper I kept folded up in my purse, away from everyone but myself and God.

Three weeks after I made the commitment to pray in the chapel every Thursday, I got a call from my doctor. I had been traveling for work and was driving back from Kansas City after a two-day teaching conference I had conducted for my clients.

"Crystal, have you ever thought about adoption?" he began.

"Why do you ask?" I replied.

He went on to tell me that he had been on call at the hospital and had delivered a baby at 6 o'clock that morning. During labor, the mother had asked that he find the baby a good mother, and said that she had decided to give the baby a better home than she felt she could provide. He added that the decision needed to be made right away and that the baby would find a home fast because there were parents on waiting lists all over.

I asked, "Why did you think of calling me?"

"I don't know why, but you were just the first person that came to my mind at the time," he answered.

I became concerned. I told him I didn't know how I would explain this to my husband at such short notice. He replied that he had already called and talked to him earlier that day, and that my husband told him to call me. I knew that it was a done deal.

I became a mother that very day. Granted, there was a lot of paperwork to be done. It took ten days, but the process was started, and it was **easy**. Just as I had requested in the prayer I wrote down on paper.

We were able to bring her home on a Friday evening. The next Thursday, as I was getting ready to fulfill my 20 minutes of prayer at the church, I stood up with my daughter and felt woozy. Something hit me – a thought. It wasn't just a weird feeling... It was... Could I be pregnant? No way. I couldn't be! Not after trying so hard for four years straight. Not after giving up on all the crazy medical procedures. I had not felt myself lately, and had just chalked it up to not getting enough sleep with the new baby.

I took a pregnancy test. *Just for giggles*, I thought to myself. It was positive. I stood staring at it and rereading the box because I couldn't believe what I was seeing. *Maybe I was doing something wrong, or misreading it*, I thought.

I took another. It was positive.

I took another. It was positive again.

I stood in disbelief. At that very moment, I snapped out of my daze, and my eyes shot up to the clock. I was late for my 4:00 meeting with God at the chapel. I learned I was pregnant at exactly 4:00 pm on a Thursday, and it changed everything for me.

> *"Don't simply dismiss a coincidence and let it drift away. Life is totally interconnected. These unusual 'things' are simply connections that surprise you because you aren't used to seeing life except in fragments. Now it's beginning to piece itself together."*
>
> Deepak Chopra

I believe we can literally think what we want into our lives. We can pray, believe, request, and attract all that we desire. It can happen as fast as we want as long as we are ready to recognize and accept the opportunities when they present themselves. When we act with intention and clarify the desires of our hearts, we truly tap into our ability to manifest.

I urge you to become super specific about what you want and super general with your feelings surrounding it. Stop wondering how it's going to happen. Stop worrying that it won't. Stop doubting and act as if it will show up. Surrender to the fact that it will show up. Know with certainty that it will happen, and it will be your responsibility to say "Yes" when it does.

This may be an uncomfortable feeling. It was not comfortable for me to surrender to adopting. I felt like I was giving up my dream to give birth to a child. I let it go. I surrendered. I got excited about it. I let it in. I stopped caring about **how** I was going to have a child. I just said, "Show me the baby."

I had been trying so hard that I was inviting resistance and frustration into my life. It was not easy for me to say, "Show me the baby and I will adopt." I had to let go, and realize that my own struggle was setting up barriers of worry and shame and doubt. With every failed attempt I had grown a little more pissed off. The more jealous I grew about those septuplets, the more I set up road blocks in my mind.

I started feeling sorry for myself. I started thinking it was never going to happen for me. I felt like I was being punished. I allowed myself to feel like a victim. We all do this. We set up mental blocks – the harder we try to make something happen, the more we are setting up resistance and not allowing it to actually happen. This was definitely the case with me.

When I surrendered and acted with intention – buying the baby blanket – I was letting it happen. When I felt certain and content that it was on the way, I let in not just one baby, but two.

When I stopped calling myself infertile and thinking of myself as having an infertility problem, I became super fertile. I later became pregnant three more times. Two resulted in miscarriages, and the third brought me my third child. I have three children now, and had them all in a span of 2 years and 8 months.

Why Things Happen in Threes

Ever notice that things happen in threes? My theory is that it starts with people focusing on an occurrence and attracting additional occurrences. We attract and manifest what we think about most.

In 1998, just three weeks after my brother took his life, I was in complete emotional agony. Not only was I grieving his loss at a level I'd never experienced before, I was tormented by guilt over the last conversation I'd had with him. He was younger than I was, and I felt that I had helped raise him. I'm not going to compare losing my brother to losing a child; my point is that I felt somehow responsible. The coulda, woulda, shouldas had taken over my mind and it was torture.

At the time I was traveling a lot as a sales executive, both by car and by plane. In the span of three days I found myself in unusual situations on two separate occasions. These events were so highly unusual I can only attribute them to attraction in action.

On one evening I found myself dead center of a string of tornados in Iowa. I managed to drive my way out of danger at over 90 miles an hour in complete darkness. Other people on the road had decided to abandon their cars and dive for nearby ditches. My instincts told me to turn my car around and beat the tornados that I could literally see following me in my rearview mirror. I made it to safety, but less than 48 hours later I had another strange encounter.

I was on another interstate, driving through the state of Illinois. A man's hat had blown away, and he had pulled off to the side of the road to retrieve it and decided to walk right out in front of my car to cross the road. I was able to come to a screeching halt, but I will never forget my horror at what came next. The car behind me was unable to stop, swerved to avoid hitting my car, and hit the man at 60 miles an hour, throwing him up into the air like a rag doll. He landed on the hood of my car before rolling off onto the road in front on me. I was in shock. A person usually only sees this type of carnage in action movies. I saw it up close and very personal. The poor man was pronounced dead at the scene, and I was left with the movie playing in my head. In the span of three weeks I had learned of my younger brother's death, attended his funeral, run from a string of 19 tornados, and witnessed a man land on the hood of my car and die. I am convinced that this was *not* an accident. My mind had attracted these events.

In my grief and agony over my brother's death, I had visions of death and suffering and fear. My thoughts were dark. My mind was focused on exactly what I did not want, on worst case scenarios. The visions of my brother lying in a casket haunted me relentlessly. The ghost of death was chasing me, and I was welcoming it in.

This is what we do. We welcome in the exact things we do not want, like air traffic controllers guiding planes down a runway. We fear being late for a meeting and sure enough, every known time waster presents itself. Can't find shoes or keys, traffic is backed up to China... we create the energy that makes it happen. Our self-talk, our attitudes, and our visions create our world. There are no coincidences.

We decide to throw out a nasty comment about someone along with a strong vibration or feeling of anger, and sure enough it comes right back to us as a nasty look or heated exchange from someone later that day. Feeling misunderstood and victimized only brings more misunderstanding and victimization into our lives. Focusing on emotional drama only multiplies it, breeding crappy relationship issues like a bad soap opera from the 70s. Karma really is a bitch but we all set the stage for it, deciding exactly how much of it we want.

The Cabin

*"The monotony and solitude of a quiet life
stimulates the creative mind."*

Albert Einstein

I grew up in the Midwest. The winters were cold and long, and I always felt that I was supposed to be somewhere else. I moved to Des Moines in my early twenties, and after getting married felt that there was no way I could move away. I remember feeling envious of people who moved to warmer climates in places like San Diego or Florida. I never thought it was in the cards for me because I was shackled, living in someone else's life, doing what they wanted. Seven years after my divorce, I was ready to make serious changes but knew I was facing a challenge with my kids' father, who had shared custody. About a year before, I had asked God/the Universe to help me fall in love with Iowa so the nagging longing to move away would leave me. I knew it was causing resentment and bad feelings and knew what bad feelings would attract into my life.

One day, while browsing the web, a picture caught my eye, of a surreal-looking 4,000 square foot log home sitting on 25 acres, nestled by its very own lake. I clicked on the picture, and found out that it was for sale, but out of my price range. That didn't stop me. I inquired, and sure enough, the owner of the property was about to take it off the market and was up for leasing it. I moved in two weeks later. People call me lucky, but I honestly believe it has less to do with luck, and more to do with attracting what your heart desires, knowing that it will be there. Sometimes when you see something you feel like you would do anything for, or feel a love for that thing or experience, you must not ignore it. It means something. The desires of the heart are telling you something about yourself and what could be. What should be.

"Delight yourself in the Lord, and he will give you the desires of your heart."

Psalm 34:4

Living in the enormous log home felt like living in a lodge built for 25 people. The place was full of windows that overlooked the beauty of Iowa: rolling green prairies as far as the eyes could see, beautiful deer and other critters running around all the time. As much as I'd always loved adventures and trips to Italy, Bermuda, and Maui, this place was one of the most unbelievable places I'd ever known. I felt like I'd placed an order and God had handed it to me, once again. I spent months soaking up the place and its treasures with my kids, as we kayaked on the lake, built fires for s'mores, and played with the four-wheelers on Saturdays. Then the winter finally kicked in, and I felt like I was locked away, surrounded by snow. One morning, as snow piled up around the windows, with more snow on the way, I realized I was going to be snowed in for a few days. I've never liked to feel snowed in or unable to get out. I took long walks in the snow and used the time to connect with nature and reflect. I wrote a large part of this book that winter. The quiet of the country was something I'd never experienced and I realized it was also helping me quiet my own mind. There is something to be said for quieting the mind and listening to your heart.

While living in the big cabin, there were several moments I felt closer to God than ever. I believe he talks to us if we listen. We just have to invite him in. I've always struggled with quieting my mind, but that's where true bliss lies for me. I used the time to create and ended up creating programs for my business and implementing ideas that I'd not been able to before. This led to a flurry of creation, but it also led to problems with my finances.

I was still trying to do too much alone, and had taken on too much work with clients. I felt like a workaholic; I was asking too much of myself and I knew it. I hadn't realized, though, just how much responsibility I'd taken on, and I was learning painful lessons about clients and how they could take advantage of my time if I let them.

One client (whom I'd taken on against my instincts) was putting a lot of pressure on me and causing resentment in my heart. I couldn't confront him, and I realized I did not know how to handle this guy. At the time I was still trying to finish my book, traveling for speaking engagements, marketing my online business practically by myself, and writing for others, all while being a mother to three children and paying for this amazing cabin I was leasing. It was all too much, and I knew that something had to give. At times I was only getting about four hours of sleep per night.

This client was contacting me with requests non-stop, and was taking more of my time than he deserved or ever paid for. I felt responsible for his inability to get the work done that I was coaching him to do, so I would do it for him. Big mistake! And big lesson learned. One night after I'd worked with him for months, he decided to do a chargeback for thousands of dollars despite the hours upon hours I'd spent working for him on his projects.

Then another series of financial events piled up, and I was in big trouble. Another client cancelled and was unable to pay her invoice or fulfill her contract. Another client started paying late and asked for a payment option that cut into my cash-flow. I began focusing on the problems surrounding me, overwhelmed by it all, and let fear set in. I felt isolated and trapped.

My merchant account had shut down due to the chargeback, and my cash flow had come to a sudden, shrieking halt. Another merchant account put a hold on funds for several months and I seemed to be unable to do anything about it.

In a panic, I decided to do the only thing I knew to do, and that was take on even more work – but even that seemed to have dried up. I could no longer focus on what needed to happen and I was unable to create the required marketing content. Fear does that to us. It robs us of our ability to create. I let worry set in. I'm not usually a worrier but this time I let it in. It controlled me and my creative ideas shut down along with everything else.

One night when I'd finally had enough, I broke down crying, which is rare for me. I felt like I had surrounded myself with snow, clients, work, and an overwhelming amount of responsibility. I remember feeling like giving up. I let those old feelings of unworthiness set it. I started feeling like I wasn't worthy to live in such an amazing place. Who did I think I was living in such an expensive place? Creepy, soul-crushing words I used to hear from my mother seeped in. "Why so big?" "You're just trying to be something you're not." "If everyone knew the real you, they wouldn't like you so much."

I felt defeated. I felt alone. I felt like I didn't have the answers anymore. I had lost sight of what I was going for and the lights were getting dimmer and dimmer on the journey.

At the height of my loneliness I cried out for God to just tell me what to do and I remembered what I'd always heard from others in past jobs and other circumstances. "You always seem to think you have to do it all yourself." Then it hit me. I needed to surrender, which was something that I was never good at. I know we are supposed to let go of the worry and surrender to God, and so I did. I let go and totally surrendered. I asked God to show me the way, and trusted he would supply me with answers.

At that very moment – literally seconds later – I heard a knock at the door. This freaked me out – no one had ever knocked on the door of the cabin. I never had visitors that I hadn't expected.

I was almost embarrassed to answer the door because my face was covered with tears and mascara, and I felt like a mess. I'll never forget that moment as long as I live, though. It was the owner of the property, and he was crying too. A grown man stood there crying in front of me, and as I wiped my tears away I didn't even know what to say other than, "Are you okay?" I can't even remember the last time I'd witnessed a man cry. I'd never been around men who showed their emotions like this.

He asked me the same thing and stepped in. He immediately said that he had something amazing to tell me. He went on to describe what had happened to him just moments earlier before knocking on the door. He said that he had just been cured of cancer and that he had come out to the cabin because he always felt closer to God when he was closer to nature. For years he had been battling skin cancer and driving to Mayo for treatments.

He had been scared that it had come back and drove out to the cabin to find peace. Just moments before knocking on the door, he felt the presence of God in a way he had never felt before. He surrendered to God, and God gave him a sense of peace that overwhelmed him – he felt it from the top of his head down, like a lightning bolt through his body. He was so moved that he wanted to tell me about it. He said that God told him to share the story with me and that everything was going to be okay.

He went on to admit that he didn't know exactly why he was telling me this or why he felt so compelled to do so, but when he saw that I was crying when I opened the door he couldn't hold back. He explained that he was not a churchgoing man himself and hadn't gone for years. He handed me a book and told me to read it. We ended up talking for hours about his experiences over the last two years, with cancer and a near-death experience.

It was my moment of white flag surrender that had attracted this experience. I'm convinced that when we totally surrender to God and the Universe and send out vibrations of complete belief that the answers are on the way, our problems will be solved... there will be a response. Not always as vivid, bizarre, and literal as a knock on the cabin door, but the quieter you become and the more you believe and submit, the more pronounced, obvious, and clear-cut the sign will be.

My trials and tribulations have always involved a struggle to surrender but every time I am able to do it, it pulls me through. The more I embrace that spirit of surrender, the easier things seem to come. I share this with you because it's important. If you are trying to accomplish big things in your life you will find it easier if you can surrender in faith.

*"Just trying to do something – just being
there, showing up – is how we get braver.
Self esteem is about doing."*

Joy Browne

Learn to work hard to prove you want it, but do not forget to surrender and listen to Spirit because that will be what pulls you through. It's called Moxie. Moxie is Faith in Action.

Many times in my life I've acted on impulse and that hasn't always worked out well for me, but whenever I've listened to Spirit and worked hard and surrendered when necessary, Spirit has never let me down. I have never been proved wrong that there is something out there looking out for me. Know it and believe it deep down. The good news is that we all have access to it.

I've become more and more convinced by my experiences that I cannot ignore this power. I've learned there are no straight lines. The road to financial freedom and happiness is a long winding one, full of bumps and hairpin turns. It gets dark sometimes and you have to squint to see the signs, and you will feel lost and scared, and you will feel exhausted and want to cry. You will pass others along the way who will point and look at you as if you're crazy and you will have to steer clear of them and hold on to faith with determination and vision even when no one else can see it.

On the surface, people may think that things just happen to me or that I'm lucky. The truth is that that most of the time there is almost always something wacky going on behind the scenes. I've come to realize that most people are not equipped to handle everything that goes on behind the scenes, and will avoid it at all costs. Those wacky times – doing things most people won't do – make me stronger. They prove to me that I'm on the right track. When I've stayed up all night to finish a chapter or hit a deadline, or when I've stretched my belief in something and actually hit a money goal, that's when I confirm that I've got what it takes. Everyone does – they just lack faith.

There are times I feel blessed that I'm strong enough to handle the rocky, wacky, winding road. And then there are times I fear I've lost all faith. We all do that when we're reaching new heights we've not reached before. That's when I turn to Spirit and hold on for dear life. I sometimes envision myself hanging on the side of a cliff with my nails, clawing my way to the top, because that's what it feels like.

In business I like to describe God/Spirit as my project manager. Even though I'm in charge of the vision, when I hand over the project management position to God it infuses me with a faith that pulls it all together. I've also learned to accept and understand that the journey won't always look the way we want it to look when we arrive.

We are all qualified to succeed by our faith and what we say yes to, not by our degrees or abbreviations after our names. The opportunities we take on determine our competence and adequacy.

Believe in Angels

*"God's angels often protect his people from
potential enemies."*

Billy Graham

Over the years I've often thought that I must have an angel by my side. Some "superpower" right there, ready to protect me from harm. I like to think of angels as muses because they inspire me as well. I'll get flashes of insight about a person or pick up intuitive energy about a coincidence. I see them as signs from God.

I'm not the only one. Kabbalah describes angels as bundles of light, meaning intelligence and consciousness. Kabbalists believe that everything has above it an angel inspiring it to change, grow, and evolve.

I've felt like angels were right there shielding me from harm too many times to count. In 1984 my family and I missed a horrible massacre by just 24 hours. It happened in San Diego, and I will never forget that day. We had been traveling to visit family in California and we stopped at a McDonald's. In the same restaurant the next day, a gunman opened fire killing 21 people and injuring dozens of others.

On another occasion, in 1997, I walked away practically unscathed from a head-on collision – even the EMTs noted how freaky it was. It was a freezing cold night, and I was driving to Minneapolis on my way to a business meeting the next morning – something I felt like I just had to attend for work. I was taking college classes and didn't want to miss a particular class so I left later than I wanted to, even though I knew the weather was getting bad. This was normal for the Midwest and I'd had plenty of experience driving in snow storms and icy conditions. It didn't stop me. I figured I'd see how it went, and would pull off the road if I felt like it was too bad to continue. I can still remember standing in the icy campus parking lot after class, unable to insert my key into the frozen locks on my sporty red Nissan 240sx. I cupped my hands around the key and held it up to my mouth to breathe warmth onto it and break through the ice in the lock.

After a couple of hours on the road, I felt like the road was safe enough. I had another two hours to go. I was looking forward to staying at the Ritz, in warmth and luxury. As I got closer to Minneapolis I watched for my exit, looking up as each exit sign approached. I had just fueled up and was stepping out of the car. The temperature was a fierce 30 below zero with the wind chill. I was regretting having misplaced my gloves. Cold air at that temperature can make your skin go into shock, fast.

Just moments after I got back on the road I saw the glare of white lights on the road ahead of me completely illuminating my view. Nothing but headlights to tell me what was about to take place. My Nissan had automatic seat belts connected to the door that zipped up and around your body as you shut the door, but the lap belt was optional. I had opted out, so the shoulder strap was the only thing keeping me safe and intact.

I'd always been a quick thinker, able to move fast and make decisions quickly enough. But not this time. A split second of sheer terror ripped through my mind instead. My life flashed before my eyes. No time to hit the brakes. No time to swerve. The moment was already upon me. I will never forget how many thoughts fit into that one second. Then the crushing, grating, jagged sound of metal on metal.

I was immediately and completely filled with regret. I regretted every moment I'd taken for granted and every word I'd held back. I resented the thought that this was really it. It hit me that this was going to happen, and an intense feeling of sadness rushed over me. I remember thinking, *This is how it's going to end? Really? Like this?* I regretted the moments I was not going to have to say goodbye, and the fact that I'd not had children yet. I regretted so much. Time seemed to stand still, until it eventually collapsed into a rush of reality. I struggled to breathe.

Glass everywhere. Somehow my legs had decided to rise up and I was pushing up against the dashboard with them as I fought to take that breath. It seemed like forever before I could finally gasp in that first breath. And then a man appeared suddenly outside the car door and reached in. He took my hand in his to keep it warm. He didn't ask if I was okay; he just kept assuring me I was. I found that most comforting because I was not sure I was; I still thought I might be dying. He just kept chanting this and telling me that help was on the way. He was breathing his warm breath on my hand to keep it from freezing in the crazy subzero wind.

He was an angel. They usually come in the form of people. I told him that I couldn't breathe and my chest hurt. I was afraid to look down because I had convinced myself there was something wedged in my chest – something like the steering wheel or an engine part. The heaviness was unreal and it hurt like hell to take in each breath. He told me everything was fine, that I'd just had the wind knocked out of me – that my seat belt had likely broken a rib or two, but it was nothing they couldn't fix.

I was suddenly relieved and looked down. He was right. There was nothing jutting out of my chest. I was intact. My limbs were all there. My breathing got a little easier and I became aware of how cold it was.

Next came the Jaws of Life, literally – that hydraulic tool that pulls and cuts away metal to rescue people from mangled cars was tearing at my car to rescue me, like a celestial being delivering me from destruction and into the light.

Not only do angels and muses show up to guide us and protect us, they are making magic happen behind the scenes. Even though we control much of our destiny with our thoughts and fantasies, we are also led to answers. I think W.H. Murray says it best in *The Scottish Himalayan Expedition*:

> Concerning all acts of initiative (and creation) there is one elementary truth, the ignorance of which kills countless ideas and splendid plans: that the moment one definitely commits oneself, then providence moves too. All sorts of things occur to help one that would not otherwise have occurred. A whole stream of events issues from the decision, raising in one's favour all manner of unforseen incidents and meetings and material assistance which no man would have dreamed would come his way. I have learned a deep respect for one of Goethe's couplets: "whatever you can do, or dream you can, begin it. Boldness has genius, magic, and power in it. Begin it now."

Unleash Your Moxie

Business Moxie

Consistency Breeds Credibility – Show Up for 21 Days

"A goal is like a strenuous exercise – it makes you stretch."

Mary Kay Ash

Consistency breeds credibility. In business, in life... everywhere. Bad habits seem hard to break, but in reality it just takes about 21 days to chuck a bad one or start a new one. Whether it's a junk food eating habit, a bad money-spending habit, or a habit of being a bully with your inner self-talk, get Moxie with it. Be proactive. Get a little tough, but use self-talk that will actually encourage you.

Only 10% of people control the wealth in this world. I attribute this to one thing: habits. Most people don't know how to break a bad habit or how to focus their intentions on creating new ones. But if I can do what I've been able to do with three kids in tow and no good role model for most of my life (in either health or wealth) you can too. It just takes a persistent mindset hell-bent on getting what you want. And it all starts with adding a few habits to your daily life.

I did not have any entrepreneurs or business-minded people in my life growing up, or even in my early twenties. I never started working out or eating healthy until I was in my late twenties. My grandparents died of smoking related deaths in their fifties. As idiotic as this sounds, I started smoking in my early twenties and as I only kept it up for about two years, I did eventually quit. It was very hard. I had to talk myself through it every day and manage my stress while I did. I had to find ways to make it work. I documented every day, and it took me exactly 21 days to completely kick the habit. The first three days were very, very hard. The next 10 days were easier. The remaining days were not so bad, but I had to stay away from other smokers just like I stay away from weak people now when it comes to other areas of my life.

My grandfather lived with us for a short while before he died. I would fall asleep listening to him at night, connected to an oxygen tank, struggling to breathe. My father was an alcoholic and even after joining Alcoholics Anonymous a few times, he picked the habit back up, even though he has diabetes and heart disease and is at least a hundred pounds overweight. He has let resistance and old self-sabotaging behaviors win, while he chooses to lose. Most of my family members are overweight. I do not know anyone in my immediate family who gets any real exercise consistently or eats healthy as a way of life.

It is imperative that you don't pick up the bad habits of others through osmosis. The five people you spend the most time with are the people you are going to become most like. Write those people's names down and ask yourself if you want to become them. Those five people will shape who you become. You will attract the same characteristics, the same attitudes, and in so doing you will begin attracting the kind of lives they lead. Even if you say you don't want it, that won't stop it from happening. You will still attract it. It's a law.

I did not fall in love with running right off the bat. I hated it at first. Then I tolerated it. Then I fell in love with the feeling it gave me. I'm convinced that if you keep anything up for 21 days, really focus, and test, track, and tweak what you're doing, you can create just about any habit.

According to Tom Corley, author of *Rich Habit: the Daily Success Habits of Wealthy Individuals*, there are 20 habits you should consider, based on what the wealthy do that the poor do not. Notice that health and wealth go hand in hand:

1. 70% of wealthy people eat less than 300 junk food calories per day. 97% of poor people eat more than 300 junk food calories per day.
2. 23% of wealthy people gamble. 52% of poor people gamble.
3. 80% of wealthy people are focused on accomplishing some single goal. Only 12% of the poor do this.
4. 76% of wealthy people exercise aerobically four days a week. 23% of poor people do this.
5. 63% of wealthy listen to audio books during commute to work. 5% of poor people do.

6. 81% of wealthy people maintain a to-do list. 19% of poor people do.
7. 63% of wealthy parents make their children read two or more non-fiction books a month. 3% of poor people do this.
8. 70% of wealthy parents make their children volunteer 10 hours or more a month. 3% of poor people do this.
9. 80% of wealthy people make Happy Birthday calls. 11% of poor people do.
10. 67% of wealthy people write down their goals. 17% of poor people do.
11. 88% of wealthy people read 30 minutes or more each day for education or career reasons. 2% of poor people do this.
12. 6% of wealthy people say what's on their minds. 69% of poor people do.
13. 79% of wealthy people network five hours or more each month. 16% of poor people do.
14. 67% of wealthy people watch one hour or less of TV every day. 23% of poor people do.
15. 6% of wealthy people watch reality TV. 78% of poor people do.
16. 44% of wealthy people wake up three hours before work starts. 3% of poor people do.
17. 74% of wealthy people teach good daily success habits to their children. 1% of poor people do.
18. 84% of wealthy people believe good habits create opportunity and luck. 4% of poor people do. 76% of wealthy people believe bad habits create bad luck. 9% of poor people do.
19. 86% of wealthy people believe in lifelong educational self-improvement. 5% of poor people do.
20. 86% of wealthy people love to read. 26% of poor people do.

The question becomes: How bad do you want to succeed?

If it takes just 21 days to change a habit and get you on the right track, why aren't you putting that on your calendar and ramping up for a real change? Do it. Get busy with it. Plan it out and consider the next 21 days your 21 steps to freedom – freedom from the prison your habit has had you locked up in. This is a chance to kick it and start finally living again, a way to tell the Universe you are choosing a better path, and telling it where you want it to lead you.

Be Moxie about it. Don't put it off. Take the reins and begin now.

Do it now. Do it now. Do it now.

Doing it now is the only way to do it. Anything else is just the inner bitch telling you she's in charge. Remember she's a bully. Stand up and do it now.

> *"I do not wish (women) to have power over men; but over themselves."*
>
> Mary Wollstonecraft

> *"From birth to 16 a girl needs good parents, from 16 to 30 good looks, from 30 to 50 a good personality and 60+ she needs good cash."*
>
> Sophie Tucker

Less Is More in Business and in Life

When I was younger I thought a full schedule, loaded with social activities, meant that I was liked. I thought that having a lot of friends meant I was somehow desirable and cool. I loved jewelry and clothes, and later on in my twenties, I couldn't buy enough of them. I was known for wearing the best suits and snappy shoes when I was working at my stuffy office job at an insurance company.

I didn't have these things as a kid, and even remember being picked on for wearing hand-me-downs or for only owning one pair of jeans or shoes. I never wore the latest trendy clothes unless I borrowed them from a friend's closet. I tried to make up for it later. When I got my first credit card at age 18, I bought a new wardrobe. "The more, the merrier" was my attitude, both in my closet and on my calendar. The more shoes I had, the more tolerable it was getting up in the morning to go to my dead end job. The more parties I was attending, the better I could tolerate the rest of my life.

A lot of us think and live this way. Don't get me wrong. I'm not condemning having nice things. I actually believe the nicer your house, the smarter you are, because you can write off a portion of it in taxes when you use your home to entertain clients. Wearing nice clothes gives us confidence and helps our positioning. I believe you need to walk your talk too. I've said many a time that "clothes open doors." I used to be baffled when I'd see a sales girl I worked with wear questionable casual clothes to her sales appointments. I knew she wasn't impressing the higher level clientele – the ones who could pay their invoices on time and buy larger contracts. She struggled, and I knew her attire was part of the reason.

Before I start to sound too much like I'm contradicting myself, let me get to my main point – that less is more.

When it comes to business, less is more productive. Doing less is actually creating more. Let me expand on this – it's an understanding that will change your life.

Too much clutter clutters your mind. You can't get clarity or focus with a cluttered mind. It's all rooted in fear – fear of letting go, fear of not being enough, fear of not having enough. Clear your space and your calendar of clutter, and only allow time and space for what is important. This will actually give you a ton more time in your life.

A lot of my clients don't have the ability to clear their own schedules at first. They've conditioned themselves to think that busy work and fully loaded homes, garages, and appointment books are what will bring them fulfillment. It's actually the other way around. Overloading our space and our time is actually exhausting us mentally and spiritually, and keeping us feeling like something is missing. It can even make us feel as if we're doing something wrong, at which point we add even more to our schedules. We just keep piling it on. It's a hamster wheel that we keep running on, getting nowhere.

Everything is energy. Clearing the clutter in your life and schedule will make way for more energy, vitality, and money. I promise you.

Karen Kingston wrote a little book called *Clearing the Clutter with Feng Shui*, and it's worth reading. You can read it in one sitting, and get a whole new outlook on life if you do what she says to do. You may find it so motivating that you're clearing out the clutter in your home even before you get to the end of the book.

Scarcity mindsets are almost always coupled with useless clutter. Those clothes that I'd collected and clung to for years (even though I wasn't wearing most of them) are a perfect example. I would forget that most of them were there because they were packed so deep in my closet I couldn't get to them. I was holding on to them because of a lie – the lie that somehow those clothes couldn't be replaced. What I didn't realize was that, by holding on to all those clothes, I wasn't making room for anything else.

If you want more of the good stuff to come into your life, you'll have to get rid of the old stuff you're not using. If you need more money, clear the decks and it will come in.

If you feel like you're too busy with your business, more often than not your bank account is empty. When your schedule is overloaded you're operating in reactive mode. This is not good for business. When you're in reactive mode, you're just getting by – just keeping your head above water. You'll never get ahead like that. Get your positioning straight and your marketing all planned out ahead of time, and you will begin operating in proactive mode, instead of reactive mode. In proactive mode, you can begin to have more time and money than you've ever had in your life.

The excuses are lies too. If you think you can't clear your schedule, you've bought a lie that has you stuck in reactive mode and keeps you from changing your situation. I have three kids and ran my business from home most of the time when I started out. There are a ton of excuses we make up in our heads and condition ourselves to believe. We get conditioned by our own experiences and the experiences of those around us. If you didn't have entrepreneurs and problem solvers in your family growing up, you will not have this naturally conditioned way of thinking. The good news is you can reprogram your mind. You just need to be aware of the thoughts and beliefs that are limiting you, and focus on getting intentional with your actions.

Doing less gives you opportunities to focus on the more important income-producing activities that are vital to your business. The activities that promote growth and freedom. The activities that grow your database, your sales, and your income.

There is an important concept that took me several years to understand because I had conditioned myself to believe that everything was hard and a struggle. Here's the concept I want you to embrace and take with you:

It's harder to struggle than it is to be successful.

This way of thinking will change your life. You'll find that it's dead-on super truth. Your life will get easier, smoother, and more abundant when you start changing the way you think, and start living this on a cellular level. At first it will seem a like a fantasy. Keep thinking it, though, and you'll start to believe it because you'll start seeing the truth of it in subtle ways. You may start getting unexpected checks in the mail. You'll feel luckier. You'll get the parking space in the spot you wanted. You'll get more clients who seem effortless to work for. What is really happening is that your mindset is changing – you're starting to let things into your life.

More than once in my life (and especially in my business) I've experienced a whole string of what seems like bad luck coming from all angles. A fender bender will lead to an extra bill, which will lead to a client being a pain the butt, ending in a seeming flurry of really bad luck... And then I'll remember that every time my business is upleveling or changing, I need to change with it. The string of bad luck is coaxing me to uplevel and release some tasks from my calendar or let a particular client go. I need to release the old, and let in the new. As your business grows, you'll notice this too. I'm warning you that if you don't become aware of this and start making positive changes – releasing the old to make way for the new – it can take you down.

Trim the Fat

> *"Clutter is not just physical stuff. It's old*
> *ideas, toxic relationships and bad habits.*
> *Clutter is anything that does not support*
> *your better self."*

Eleanor Browne

The secret to boosting your bottom line and getting more cash flowing in is to get rid of the old and let in the new ideas and opportunities.

When you trim the fat in your surroundings and business, you boost your bottom line.

When I'm feeling stuck or stagnant and need a new rush of inspiration, clients, or good hard cash, I start chucking the old files, ideas, and products that didn't work or aren't working. We've all got ideas that either flopped or never came to fruition for whatever reason, right? Well, that old junk needs to find its way to the trash bin so it doesn't clutter your hard drive or office space. I'm not just talking about hard copy files and remnants of last year's ad copy flyers; I'm talking about whatever is within your field of vision. Feeling stuck and stagnant almost always comes with cluttered, stuck, and stagnant surroundings. And that includes relationships.

Well, sometimes the best thing to do is show them the door. This allows good energy to start flowing in and will actually work internally to free space in your mind for creativity.

It's true. Ever hear of Aristotle's and Einstein's theory that nature abhors a vacuum? Well, physicists and philosophers today agree. When you declare your intentions, the Universe will accommodate them, but you've got to create space for it physically and mentally.

Every time I clean out my file drawers, desk top, iPhone contacts, iCalendar, or even my unused WordPress plugins, I feel energy flowing and then see it in motion with fresh ideas, new clients coming to me, and sales coming through.

Here are three areas I tell clients to start cleaning up right away when working with me:

1. File Storage

You don't need to chuck important files and records but put them in a different area, neatly organized, and only keep the absolutely crucial documents. Set up new files ready for current clients *and* new clients. Space for new higher paying clientele should be set up and neatly arranged (I like color coding my files) so that you can welcome them in. Even if higher paying $10k-20k clients are just a dream for you right now, you've got to get ready for them. When your mind and the Universe know you're not ready for higher paying clients, they don't usually come knocking. You've got to let them in by preparing for them. Create sections for them in your 3-ring binders or online file systems. Ideas for revenue-generating projects should be planned out and given time on your calendar. Any ideas that are floating out there distracting you – that you know deep down won't work or are avoiding because your heart's not really in them – chuck 'em!

2. Website Clutter

A confused mind never buys. Period. Take a look at your website and decide what may be confusing, overload, or just plain distracting to your website traffic and potential customers. You want to lead your prospects to do something, to take action – not to be so overwhelmed with all of your videos, products, blog content, or web buttons that they don't know what to do first and hightail it out of there. Think about streamlining your page and directing your customers exactly where you want them to go, like a landing page to grab their email or contact information. You don't want them to land on a page with so many bells and whistles they feel like a 3-year-old on Christmas morning, playing with the box and paper and overlooking the shiny toy.

3. Relationships

We acquire new relationships every day, and let's face it: Some of our older acquaintances and even clients don't always inspire the best feelings in us. So why keep them around? Consider surrounding yourself with new, fresh faces – old and new friends who inspire you and make you want to join them in future ventures. If they inspire you or help you to reach for higher goals, even better. One client of mine had old, stale, tattered photos hanging on her office wall. The truth came out when I asked her who they were. A couple of them she no longer associated with anymore. Another was a realtor from her past career as a real estate agent, who stole her clients from her left and right, making her life miserable. Another was a past client who had recently begun suing her! How could anything good and fresh come into her life, with these pictures around, bringing up feelings of resentment and painful memories? The fastest way to attract good things is to feel good about your surroundings. The late Jim Rohn said, "You become the average of the 5 people you spend the most time with." That's not just true of flesh-and-blood people; surround yourself with visions of what you actually want to come to fruition.

Get Laser Focused So You Get Everything You Want

Let's get you laser focused; it will get you more money. Laser focus will bring you uncommon results in your business and in your life. And yes, when I say uncommon results, I'm talking uncommon revenue – in other words, more cash, darlin'. That's what I like to talk about. Making more money and creating revenue is like warm brownies during PMS.

Uncommon results means hitting your number goals every month and growing from there. I should know a thing or two about how to get focused because I've struggled with focus most of my life. As a child, I had the attention span of a gnat. I was never diagnosed with ADD (which they really didn't do back then) but frankly it's all water under the bridge anyway. Over time I picked up on what my major problem was: I liked to stare at the car accident.

You know what I mean, don't you? Don't you get annoyed when you're in a hurry and there's a car accident on the northbound side of the freeway and yet traffic is at a standstill on the accident-free southbound side? That's what's going on when you're supposed to be focused on making money, and yet at the end of the month you've not made enough (or *any*, God forbid.) You're letting yourself get distracted by the car accident.

Let's talk about our usual daily distractions first. Shiny objects, vibrating phones, chiming text messages, pings... the stream of distractions never ends. These distractions can be incessant, relentlessly taking your attention away from the project at hand, if you let them – the project that could be bringing in the big fat revenue, while you instead sit answering every meaningless Skype interrupt and text message that comes in.

Ladies, there are emotional and time vampires out there just yearning to suck the time and attention out of the very veins trying to bring you cash. That project needs your undivided attention to be completed, and it means the difference between your business growing or collapsing. There is much to do with an online business, and managing it can feel like sitting in the middle of Grand Central Station. It may seem impossible but it's not. You've got to unleash some restraint on all that noise.

The truth is most of it can wait. If you've got the systems in place with your business, you shouldn't feel the need to stop and give your attention to every ping, ding, or message that intrudes upon your day.

Here are a few tips that can help you get laser focused and get uncommon results in your business:

Set a timer, use a calendar, and start scheduling every minute.

When you do this, the amount of time you have available will swell. You'll feel a ton better and be *much* more profitable. It may sound ridiculous, but when you make a habit of scheduling, people will begin respecting your time. When you respect your time, others do as well. We train others how to treat us, and our time is our most valuable asset.

Your day will go smoother, your systems will run smoother, and everything will flow better: more sign-ups, more traffic, and more opportunities to get in front of the right customers. You will attract other people who run their lives and businesses like this, which leads to a whole host of positive results, including loving what you do. When you work with happy people, it affects your entire life.

When I started my coaching business, I learned the hard way just how people can suck your time if you let them. I wanted my clients to succeed so bad I would let some of them waste my time by making me repeat myself over and over, or I would give in to their need for attention or their need to vent. It cost me thousands of dollars. I soon realized that some people will never succeed because they are chronic time-wasters and self-saboteurs. I also realized that letting them waste my time was not only rude to me, it was unfair to them. I wasn't showing them the proper way to run their lives. As a coach, I have to lead by example. Getting tough about my time was one of the hardest lessons I've had to learn, but it was the most productive, once I got the hang of it.

Once I started taking my time seriously, I began attracting the kinds of clients that made the difference between $2,000 a month and $30,000. When you command control of your time, you will create a top-shelf kind of life, and you will be in greater demand. You will attract the kinds of clients who are willing and able to pay more for your services.

Turn your phone off for a couple of hours a day.

When you turn the noise off, you are preparing yourself to get mentally focused on that one project or task at hand. When you are only halfway focused, you will notice it in your bottom line. Things won't get finished, you'll appear inconsistent and sloppy, and you'll likely turn off the very customers you are trying attract. It shows. People will notice, whether you think they will or not.

Devote a laser focus weekend or week to planning.

This is *huge*. It will change your life and your business. For those small business owners and service professionals flying solo, this can literally double or triple your monthly revenue.

Here's what I mean: decide to focus on numbers, on what it will take to achieve those numbers with your marketing. Plan out your marketing well in advance with your product launches each quarter and completely plan out all your blog topics, email sequencing, social media postings, sales pages, etc. Lay it all out in detail. Break it down into monthly, weekly, and daily tasks, and then stick to that calendar. If you do this, you'll hit your goals faster than ever before.

Your World Is a Reflection of Your Own Self-Worth

I am often surprised by how many people start out in business online thinking small, pricing small, and exhausting themselves trying to sell a $47 ebook. It's no wonder they give up too soon. Who in their right mind could sustain any level of enthusiasm for hard work if they walk away with $47 at the end of the day? I've sat listening to long drawn out excuses, as they defend the strategy of starting out with a low price point product or program. I've listened to a personal friend – someone I truly care about – exhaust herself assuring me that her goal of selling a million units would work, and would generate recurring income for her. It was painful to listen to. The saddest part of this was that she had been struggling for years, and continued to stay stuck because she was in denial about the truth.

There is a way to work much smarter. Really.

Listen to me: Most of the problem doesn't lie in the $47 product, or even your strategy for selling the $47 product.

The problem is much deeper within you.

It's self-worth. I recently made a $40k sale over the phone without even having met the potential client, who was on the other side of the globe. It's all about self-worth. Here are a few things that can contribute to a low-price mentality:

You've never had a millionaire mentor or a family member with a millionaire mindset.

Your mindset, values, and self-worth were determined as a child, many years ago, under the influence of the people around you. It's not your fault; it's just a fact. You were conditioned to think like a lower or middle class income earner. Most people were. The people around you likely even threw in a few negative ideas about money and people with money – ideas that reinforced the conditioning, leading to guilt and shame around having money. The mind does not just change overnight. That's why the woman I mentioned above vehemently defended her view about working hard for a $47 sale. She's convinced herself it will work when it hasn't worked for the past four years. She's stuck there, and too stubborn to listen to any sort of logic. The enemy is deep in her subconscious mind, setting limits on her profits. The enemy is that little voice that has told her that her time's not worth more than $47 – that *she's* not worth more than $47.

You believe that making money is difficult.

You believe that making an honest living comes with grit, grime, and intense struggle. Complaining, standing all day on sore feet, working through the headache for long hours and very low wages... Sound familiar? Yep, I've heard it too, along with statements like "Money doesn't grow on trees." I grew up around this thinking. This struggle mentality was handed down from generation to generation, and it only stops when you decide to think differently, to realize it's not really helping anyone to continue struggling. Seriously, how many struggling factory workers really get to live their dreams of helping someone in Africa, or building a new school in Haiti? Not many that I've ever heard of.

You have a do-it-yourself mentality.

You may have taken this thinking on from the people around you as well. I know I was once ridiculed by a family member for hiring a housekeeper. She was very hostile about it, and I know it was coming from her own feelings and the mental conditioning that came from our grandparents. This mentality doesn't help you, because if you're doing everything yourself, you're never going to grow your business, much less your bank account. Without proper help in your business, you will stagnate, exhaust yourself, and get nowhere fast. This is sad. It's well known in business circles that hitting $300k will give your business a serious boost, because it happens to be the number that allows you to get the proper help in your business. It will ultimately help you put money back into your business, and you'll find yourself less stressed, working a lot less, and finally feeling the financial freedom everyone talks about.

The hard work is all mental. You need to re-condition yourself, and realize you are not a commodity and were never meant to be.

Your time is worth more.

You are unique and rare.

Time with loved ones was not meant to be limited to a few minutes slipped in on a holiday break. You were meant to travel, to have peace of mind, and to leave a legacy to your children so they too know how to ask for top dollar.

Test, Track, Tweak: The Power of Measurement

"Measurement is the first step that leads to control and eventually to improvement. If you can't measure something, you can't understand it. If you can't understand it, you can't control it. If you can't control it, you can't improve it."

H James Harrington

"The only man who behaves sensibly is my tailor; he takes my measurements anew every time he sees me, while all the rest go on with their old measurements and expect me to fit them."

George Bernard Shaw

Measurement. How else do we get anything done? Most people do not truly understand measurement or take the act of measurement seriously. And this is precisely why achieving their desires feels impossible. When we measure and break down goals, desires, and tasks, we achieve the impossible and overcome the insurmountable. We have historical proof of the power of measurement, yet most of us struggle every day and never get what we want because we continue to underestimate it.

The metric system is a great example of the inescapable need to measure. Currency, trade, weights and measures – the purpose of measurement is to organize an essential part of an economy: growth. Without measurement, we are at a standstill.

Goals

Earl Nightingale says a man without a goal is like a ship without a rudder.

I like to talk about the P.O.A. or Plan of Attack. It works with any type of goal. Whether the purpose is to lose weight, make more money, market a product, build a personal investment portfolio, or win an Olympic gold medal, you have to start with a Plan of Attack. Anything can be broken down into measurable steps. Not only does it work – it can work fast.

Counting numbers and measuring tasks may sound mundane and mind numbing, but if you do it right it can create a sense of momentum and immediate accomplishment. We don't like the thought of living our lives measuring everything. I heard it over and over again while working in the weight loss industry: People would tell me they didn't want to start counting and measuring calorie intake because they were afraid of developing an obsession or an unhealthy mental fixation. I say, get obsessed! How do you think Henry Ford achieved what he did with very little education? People said he was obsessed and unable to talk of much other than his car. It worked for him. We don't hear much talk of his unhealthy fixation these days, do we?

Call it obsession, call it an unhealthy fixation, call it whatever you want – I call it the drive behind an action plan. And I call the lack of measurement laziness. Measurement is the **only** way we as a species have ever accomplished anything. We've built skyscrapers, thriving economies, and pyramids; sent astronauts to the moon; and cured diseases – all by the power of intentional measurement. How do you think Edison, Bell, and Franklin achieved such monumental advancements? If they hadn't measured at every step, we wouldn't have light, telecommunication, or electricity today.

The word *goal* is overused and, in my opinion, has lost its power to create a sense of urgency. Most of us don't take it seriously. We might take a "goal" seriously at first, but as the days and weeks go by, it still remains just a "goal."

Instead of setting goals, create a "Plan of Attack." Thinking of your goals this way lends itself well to immediate results because of the nature of accomplishment – especially the big, audacious accomplishments that are worth achieving. You've got to prepare the mind, get in the groove, create that laser focus, and attack your goals!

> *"Your 'I AM' statements are more powerful than any other words because they fuel who you become and what you ultimately achieve or fail at."*
>
> Crystal O'Connor

One of my favorite lines is from the movie *The Edge*. Anthony Hopkins is mentally preparing Alec Baldwin to kill the Kodiak bear that's been chasing them through the mountains of Alaska. He makes Alec repeat over and over the line, "We're gonna kill the mother…." After repeating it several times together, you can actually feel the intense energy emerging from their repetitive mantra, the power of encouragement and the desire to live. They need that mental energy and focus to pull deep down inside them, that angry kind of energy it takes to do or accomplish great things, or – in this case – dangerous, desperate acts of survival. Anthony Hopkins' character had not only accomplished success in the business world but applied what he had absorbed in books and the boardroom to the raw, unforgiving, unexpected experience of the ruthless outdoors.

Calling your goals "POAs" will give you a renewed sense of energy, and set a fire under your tush. Sometimes that is what we need to get going and keep going toward whatever it is we want. Call it a "Plan of Attack" and see what happens inside of you. Sustaining the desire within is essential. Measurement can help with that too. Measurement enables us to see growth and results, and feed off the resulting euphoria. There is nothing quite as motivating as being able to see and track the results of your tasks, steps, and actions.

Try breaking down your tasks, and tackling them three at a time. Before you know it, your obsession will become your accomplishment.

Measure Your Time

It is amazing how willing we are to measure how much work we do ("I worked 10 hours today!") but rarely or never measure the amount of time we spend sitting in front of the TV. Have you ever heard anyone say "Gosh, I spent twelve hours aimlessly watching mindless programs and got nothing out of it?"

Measure Your Weight

Measurement is essential for results oriented weight loss, yet we often fail to understand how crucial it is. We forget – or worse, we deny – the fact that it is physiologically impossible to lose weight while taking in more calories than we expend or burn. We spend money, time, and mental energy avoiding this overwhelmingly simple fact, instead of just **measuring the darn calories**!

It is a known fact that you must burn 3,500 more calories than you take in to lose 1 pound of body fat. As indisputable as this number is, most of us do not know or have forgotten it. That magic number – 3,500 – is the formula for skinny. How can we have forgotten its relevance to weight loss? It has been known for years and yet most of us are walking around clueless about it, or so completely in denial that we blame our own metabolisms – or worse yet, genetics. We convince ourselves we have the "fat gene," that we don't really have control over our weight. But once we absorb and accept this number – 3,500 – a paradigm shift occurs within our minds and we can move forward with an action plan – a plan of measurement. And once the system starts to work, we gain our own momentum and begin to lose the weight... and it just gets easier and easier.

My client, Tammy Hardin, of The UnEmotional Eater (www.TheUnemotionalEater.com) uses EFT and other modalities to help people break past barriers and resistance with all kinds of addictions – not just eating. She specializes in all types of addiction with over 20 years of experience.

Fear of Success: Symptoms and Cures

You won't always foresee an issue until you're knee-deep in your business, you begin to grow your income, and it suddenly plateaus. You may feel stuck and unable to understand where the stagnation is coming from. You may find yourself blaming this, that, and the economy. You may need to do something different that requires you to step out of your comfort zone, but you hesitate or flat-out refuse. Maybe you are afraid of success because you fear you can't handle the responsibility or the kudos you will receive. Maybe you feel like someone in your family will judge you or call you out on your old crap, and people will find out you're unworthy.

I had many fears about writing this book even though I knew my story needed to be told. I knew it would help a lot of people – especially women – but I hesitated and procrastinated and told myself that telling these stories would ruin my life. There was a huge amount of resistance in me. I was afraid that my mother would say horrible things about me to protect her own name, that she would gather a group of women from her side of the family, that they would gang up on me and tear me to shreds online. I was afraid of the stories they would tell of how I was a bad kid – how I was caught shoplifting when I was 16 years old with a group of friends. I was afraid that would prove that I was bad, that I was a thief, and that I didn't deserve success. I feared that people would not like me or call me a horrible daughter for telling these stories, that I would be bullied by people in my family and called disloyal, and these fears stopped me.

But all of these things have already happened and I've survived. I've lived through horrible feelings of betrayal, destitution, loneliness, and being beat down. I know what feeling isolated, uncherished, and abandoned feels like. I know what it feels like not having my family around to support me – emotionally or otherwise. And I've survived. If my stories can help others feel less alone, more ambitious, and motivated to make their dreams happen, then it will all be worth it.

Most of our fears are completely irrational, based on perceptions and beliefs that were planted in our subconscious minds when we were children. These childish fears don't make sense in our adult lives.

When you come to a place where you feel stuck, you will need to begin thinking about what you want. Visualizing the outcome you want can bring you the opportunities and the answers. That's actually the easy part. The answers will always come swiftly and abundantly. You will be shown the way to your dreams and wishes like magic. It will happen in some of the most unlikely and inconceivable ways. These coincidences will seem bizarre, and when they begin to happen you will see exactly what I'm talking about.

You may be sitting in a coffee shop one morning and overhear someone telling someone else about a book or speaker that has the answer to a problem – an answer that fits like a missing puzzle piece. You might be invited to a workshop or a movie that reveals a valuable tip – something that opens up your mind and helps you understand exactly what to do next. You might get a random phone call – an opportunity to speak somewhere or address a workshop or teach a class. And someone in that audience might connect you with someone who can guide you toward your next step. You may be thinking about how to make that next sale and who your next new client will be, and the next thing you know you're standing in front of someone who needs exactly what you have to offer.

But you've got to be ready and willing to take the opportunity. When you feel too hesitant, lackadaisical, or scared to take the opportunity when it presents itself, you will know you need to build up your Moxie. This is the Saboteur rearing its ugly head.

You will need to figure it out – to ask yourself exactly where your fears are coming from and why you're not seizing the moment with Moxie. You will need to get really honest with yourself and face the fear head on in order to kiss it goodbye forever. Excuses are the disguises your fears wear. Making a list of all your fears and tackling them with brutal honesty is what will get you past them. You will see how irrational they are, and may even feel silly about them. This is progress. When your fears start to seem childish or slightly idiotic and you can laugh them off, you can begin to move forward. That's when bigger things start to happen, your income grows, your confidence builds to a new level, and you begin clearly manifesting what you want.

I see it all the time with clients who begin hitting an income ceiling in their business, don't stick with the program in their marketing calendar, or stop tracking what I'm telling them to track behind the scenes. They'll begin making up excuses – everything from not having enough time to getting stuck on a technicality or forgetting a step in the process. I always start by having my clients tell me what they want, and then when they get stuck I can remind them to go back over what we had discussed and what they were supposed to do – a task that I know would have brought them the result they were looking for. At that point, they are faced with the truth: The road to what they wanted was right there, and they chose to not move forward or to skip a step in the process or to avoid the process completely. These self-sabotaging behaviors are usually based on fear about a certain part of the process, and the key to facing that fear is in the excuse.

> *"Ninety-nine percent of the failures come from people who have the habit of making excuses."*
>
> George Washington Carver

It's time to take a look at these excuses under a microscope. Taking an honest look at the excuse usually leads to a miraculous breakthrough if the individual is ready to grow and willing to look at themselves from the inside out. For instance, if they were supposed to write a blog post about a topic we did research on and post it to a particular Facebook group with hundreds of potential clients and they didn't do it, it's time to break out the microscope. They may have put off posting to the Facebook group because they fear being judged or perceived as salesy, or even because they're afraid that their website sucks. This is usually rooted in wanting to appear perfect because anything less than perfection was punished early on in their life. They may have been rejected by someone early on and humiliated in front of strangers, resulting in a fear of being rejected in a public place like the Facebook group.

Remember that everything is within your reach. Absolutely

everything. You and you alone are the only thing standing in your way, armed with excuses and irrational fears rooted in your past experiences.

One revelation that I share with my clients who are trying to uplevel their businesses and incomes is that the one thing they least want to do is the one thing that will push them to the next level. What they most fear doing is what will bring them that $20k or $50k month. Many times the answers are staring them in the face and they can't see them because of what I call their excuse goggles. They are like beer googles but instead of seeing things from a drunk's perspective, they see them from a Saboteur's perspective. The answers are distorted, fuzzy, and unclear. You can't see the answers when you are too drunk on excuses, complaints, or feelings of low self-worth.

We usually break through this by doing a little exercise. First they write down what they already know they should be doing. Then I walk them through a process of writing down next to each avoided action the reason they haven't moved forward with it yet. Finally we walk through each reason or excuse, and we confront what's holding them back.

If the irrational fear cannot be squelched rationally, we use a more guided and therapeutic method called Emotional Freedom Technique. I have worked with several clients who are EFT practitioners and helped them with their business and marketing. I now refer other clients to them to break past these barriers. Once I discovered how amazing the results of EFT can be, I found it to be the key to unlock much of what holds my clients back in business.

Bullies

Dealing with Bullies in business is easier than you think. As uncomfortable, frustrating, and isolating as it can feel, the experience of dealing with a bully can make you stronger if you choose to understand it and take action. It's especially important to understand why bullies do what they do so that you can come from a place of acceptance and not take it too personally.

The truth is bullies pick on those who are the brightest and the best at what they do.

When you start a business, you may find yourself faced with a bully. This may prevent you from moving forward if you aren't used to it. **We can't have that.** Let me explain.

If you have ever encountered a bully, you'll notice their tactics usually center around humiliating and belittling you so as to keep you in a state of fear – the fear of losing your job, the fear of not "shining" ...it's all about keeping you in a state of inaction. Bullies seek to enslave their targets, especially when their targets attempt to preserve their dignity or their right to be treated with respect. They will employ their power and intimidation campaigns to take back control of their targets. This is because they are threatened by you because of the characteristics you possess.

I've listed below a few of the characteristics that make you a target for bullies:

- You are independent.
- You refuse to be subservient.
- You are more technically skilled than the bully.
- You are the "go-to" veteran worker to whom new employees turn for guidance.
- You are better liked by others.
- You have more social skills and possess greater emotional intelligence.
- You have empathy (even for bullies!)
- Colleagues, customers, and management (with the exception of the bullies and their sponsors) admire you and the warmth you bring to the environment.
- You are ethical and honest.
- You may be a whistle-blower who exposes fraudulent practices.
- You are not a schemer or slimy con artist.
- You believe in hard work and meeting goals.
- You have a pro-social orientation – a desire to help, heal, teach, and develop others.

It just so happens that **all of these characteristics are also**

characteristics that will take you to great levels of success in business. That is why I empower, encourage, and teach people like you to take control of your income, your life and your future by recognizing these characteristics as *leadership skills* that can lift people up, even if they are unappreciated in some corporate work environments. Turn these skills, talents, and passions into independence, wealth, and freedom, and don't let bullies hold you back.

If You're Failing to Plan, You're Planning to Fail

I'm about to give you the keys to the business kingdom. Let me tell you how I stack the odds in my favor in my business so I don't waste time, and actually make money every single week. When I started my business from scratch just three short years ago, I wasn't sure what I was going to sell or what I wanted to do. As long as I had the freedom to do *what* I wanted *when* I wanted, I figured I'd be happy.

Well, that got me *nowhere* at first. Then I had a wake-up call.

I came to realize that I had everything I needed to turn my skills and expertise into cash. At first, I was holding myself back with a terrible self-sabotaging behavior. You see, I hated planning. I always had. I *loved* freedom and thought that I could fly by the seat of my pants because I owned my own business and didn't have anyone to answer to.

Well, that first month I made nothing. Nada. Zilch. I knew that I had to do something massively different, so I borrowed a little trick that always worked in the advertising world. I'd known this little trick the whole time and just needed to implement it. And I put a plan together.

That next month I hustled with my plan. I did what I'd always known to do and I made $4,000. Looking back, I hadn't realized just how lucky I was to know exactly what to do to make $4,000 fast. Most people panic, give up, and go back to looking for a dead end job. Not everyone knows what I know. I see so many struggling, and realize that my background in sales, advertising, marketing, and education was like a recipe for rocket fuel that helped my business take off. The good news is that what I know can act as rocket fuel for *any* business, and dramatically change your life and circumstances.

Cash Flow Problems Are the Root of All Embarrassment

"The fact is that one of the earliest lessons I learned in business was that balance sheets and income statements are fiction, cash flow is reality."

Chris Chocola

Hey let's face it: Cash flow is a BIG part of a successful business. You need cash flowing into your business and bank account in nice, steady bursts. But so many small businesses struggle with this. You may be struggling with it too, especially if you're in the start-up phase.

Cash flow is money flowing in and out of your business. It flows in when customers buy your products, and out when you pay bills. More going out and less coming in creates what is known as "negative cash flow" or a "cash crunch." No fun.

Positive cash flow is then obviously when the amount coming in is more than the amount going out. Nice, right?

We all strive to balance the flow and always keep it in a positive state but realistically it's hard to do.

A solid plan helps. Here are four ways to rev up your cash flow and keep it running on all cylinders:

1. If you haven't already, create more than one income source in your business.

Without multiple income streams, you will likely run into cash flow problems consistently. This is not only stressful but it can take your business down faster than you can say "Mercy." It's completely avoidable too. Putting a plan together to create an integrated suite of products and services that create more than just one type of income is an easy answer. I teach the 30/30/30/10 income stream model.

- 30% Recurring income
- 30% Passive income
- 30% Leveraged income
- 10% Active income

This is an income stream model that opens up all kinds of revenue-generating opportunities, and when you couple it with consistent and cutting-edge marketing strategies, you can kiss your cash flow problems goodbye.

2. Take your business online so that it's marketing for you 24/7.

It's not enough to just throw up a website or blog. You need to have a plan. Plan to not only get your website up, but to keep a flow of traffic and conversations happening. This means being active and engaging, using social media, article sites, list-building options to grab emails from your traffic, product promotions, giveaways, and good content that truly helps them and will keep them coming back. You'll need to plan out your marketing calendar ahead of time so that it doesn't consume all your time. Planning out your quarter is smart, and will ignite bursts of traffic *and* cash flow by not only helping you gain active income and sales, but also creating customers for life who will keep coming, buying, and telling others about you.

3. Build a list of qualified leads and engage with them.

Use an auto-responder service to collect contact information from your visitors. This is especially important now that there are thousands and thousands of websites and so much online activity. You can cut through the clutter and stand out by staying in contact with your visitors. Grab their contact information by giving them something of extraordinary value. Be a giver. Don't hold back. It doesn't have to cost you anything – just put together some content they can put to use or will cherish. If you provide a service that helps women balance their hormones maybe you can give them an ebook, giving them ten tips to get started on the path to hormonal happiness. If you are a consultant, give them a report – really knock their socks off with your advice on whatever it is that you do. You'll be winning them over in no time and they'll remember to buy from you when the time comes to buy.

4. Raise your prices.

It's common to not charge enough. I think this is due to a common lack of knowledge regarding exactly how to position yourself in the marketplace, identify your ideal clients, and have so many customers coming to you that you begin asking what you're worth. I've found there is also a common belief regarding what people "will" pay for your services. A lot of the time when I work with someone and discuss lifting their price, we discover they have issues around money and self-worth. There is only one way to change that: good marketing and getting just *one* client to pay that higher price you never thought possible. This changes everything ...especially cash flow.

Multiple Income Streams

When I first began coaching, I was often stumped by why many of my clients would not implement what I was telling them to do. I knew that if they would just follow the steps I was telling them to take, they would get results, and grow their businesses and incomes to new levels.

I finally realized that entrepreneurs are often their own worst enemies. When an entrepreneur finds their growth stagnant, unable to get even one client, it's usually because of one of two problems. They are either doing way too much without a clear positioning statement, or they are afraid of what others will think.

Their problem was usually rooted in fear, and showing itself in what they were doing or not doing in terms of marketing. Marketing requires hustle. It requires swallowing fear of rejection and growing a tough skin. It also requires focus on one thing. One position. When you're marketing, you've got to know what your position is. Your point of view is essentially your positioning. You've got a point of view, and you need to spread the word so repetitively that you get bored with it. Yes, I'm telling you to get a little bored with your own point of view. The problem with entrepreneurs is that we get bored easily, so we want to switch things up. This isn't a good thing when it comes to your message and positioning.

I can relate, trust me. That's always been one of my own weak points. Early on in my business I'd get bored, so I'd start other projects and leave my initial projects uncompleted, because I crave newness and love the creating process.

We try too many marketing campaigns and dilute our efforts because we haven't gained any real momentum in the marketplace with our message and our positioning. I tell entrepreneurs to get used to being bored if they want success. Success is repetition to the point of boredom. Consistency breeds credibility. Your audience and prospects need to hear your message a ton. So much that it may sound overly repetitive to you and leave you feeling uninspired. Don't worry; it won't bore them. Get used to the idea of sharing your message over and over in the marketplace – really hustling with it. Set up automatic posts in software systems like Hootsuite, to go out on several social media sites for a year. Set it up and forget about it. This will help get your message out there without burning you out on it. Pick a point of view and share it often. Do it for a year. This will build a solid foundation beneath your business, and leave a healthy dose of branding in your prospects' minds.

Entrepreneurs are also known for being stubborn. Being hell-bent and never giving up is a characteristic that will get you where you want to go, however it's also a dream killer. Let me explain. When you're so stubborn you won't listen or get help with your business, it's a show stopper. Open your mind, let in the proper guidance, and you will flourish. You will need to become a master at what you do. I'm a believer in doing what you love because it will be easier to master. Malcolm Gladwell explains in his book, *Outliers*, that it takes 10,000 hours to master something – it will be much easier to put in that time if you love what you're doing.

I'm not telling you to get bogged down in mundane tasks that you can better hand off to others. I'm telling you to master the art of positioning and understand that marketing really is about redundancy and rhythm. When you're starting out and you can't hire staff yet or even a virtual assistant, you'll need to bootstrap, which means you'll need to repeat yourself. This can happen in several ways. You can be redundant in your stories, email marketing, campaigns, social media marketing, Facebook ads, the book that you write – even speaking on stage, if that is part of your marketing arsenal.

The secret of every big successful business is recurring income. I've talked about income streams from the very beginning in my business positioning, because I knew that when I was in sales, my life was easier when I sought out the bigger clients and made them happy. That way, they kept coming back for more or remained on long term contracts. That meant recurring income commissions for me.

I learned from real estate investing that life is easier when you have recurring passive income consistently flowing in. It means you can expect money well into the future, and even find yourself working less and worrying less about where your next sale will come from.

I also worked with small business ad campaigns at a TV station, and got up close and personal with their problems. I saw firsthand what small businesses struggle with the most. They struggle with cash flow and positioning. Income streams are the answer. I wanted that to be my message, because I knew I could teach it and change lives in dramatic ways.

Real estate investing is scary – it involves a lot of risk and a lot of work. When I discovered internet marketing and the power of building a list, selling information, and promoting programs and services, I liked that idea better. It seemed fun and creative, and like something I could pull off with three kids in tow.

Passive, recurring income is built on repetition and boredom – on doing something over and over again. Many clients who come to me have not nailed down their point of view or marketing yet, and think they can start bringing in passive income. Passive, recurring income is great, but it doesn't happen overnight; it's built brick by brick.

There are four income streams I teach in my programs: active, recurring, leveraged, and passive income streams. It all starts with active income – skipping the active and jumping to leveraged, recurring, and passive income is impossible. It just doesn't work that way.

Recurring and passive income are born of repetitive positioning in the marketplace and nurtured relationships. Your prospects need to know, like, and trust you before they will buy from you. Then they will need to taste test your product and know it's something they want to taste a lot before they sign up for the recurring payments that give you that recurring income.

This doesn't happen overnight, but it can happen in 12 months. What you need is to build a list of qualified leads, and you can create active income while doing this, as long as you commit to the redundancy of applying your positioning in the marketplace.

Let me explain the four types of income streams:

Active income is the income we are most familiar with; it's trading hours for dollars. This is the income you've received by working at a job since you first started working. It's the quickest and easiest type of income stream to find. You sell your time or expertise in exchange for income. It was the main income stream in my coaching business at MoxieEntrepreneur.com because it gave me instant income. I remember the first sale I made online. My client was a nutritionist who found me via Facebook, and after an online conversation she bought my six month coaching package. It involved me meeting with her once a week for an hour and teaching her how to take her business online to increase her profits. She was paying me hourly for my expertise. Looked at as an hourly rate, the coaching sessions would have broken down to something like $250 an hour.

Recurring income is an income stream that clients pay monthly. An example of recurring income in my business is my Moxie Inner Circle program. (www.MoxieInnerCircle.com) Entrepreneurs pay us $97 a month for a coaching call, a series of videos and a monthly Q&A call. The content is so good they keep paying to maintain access to it. The content helps them with the marketing and technical actions they need to take in their business, and gives them a sense of community with like-minded entrepreneurs who are focused on the same objectives. This is what I call a *low barrier to entry* program, which simply means it's giving them something that helps them get results, at a low cost that they can afford. It isn't really a new concept. You've likely paid a monthly access fee to be part of a book-of-the-month club or gym. This kind of service level is a win-win for any business. In my case, it allows me to grow my business to levels I couldn't manage with one-on-one coaching, trading hours for dollars. It's an affordable, useful service for my clients, and a good source of income for me. Think about it: if I have 200 people paying me $97 a month, that's $19,400 in recurring monthly revenue I can depend on.

Leveraged income is an income stream that involves offering services of some kind in a way that multiplies your income potential. For instance, if I'm coaching one client at $250 an hour, just imagine what kind of cha-ching comes from coaching 50 clients at once in a workshop or an advanced level coaching program. $250 becomes $12,500 an hour.

Passive income is my favorite, and it's what most entrepreneurs and small business owners come to me craving. Passive income is "making money while you sleep." It's the income that creates money over and over, long after the work is done, and it's the most appealing of the income streams. It's also the hardest to achieve, and without proper positioning and marketing it comes to nothing. It's not that passive income is a pipe dream; it's just that without that repetitive marketing early on, building a list of qualified leads, and nurturing the list, it will seem unachievable. There is a rhyme and reason to everything I teach in my programs and it's all leading toward passive income. An example of the passive income I've created in my business is my Rapid Cash Infusion program, which teaches entrepreneurs how to create quick cash in their businesses in a self-paced learning program. They get access to the program without me having to be there. It's all recorded for them and available for download after purchase.

I've worked with financial advisors, dentists, chiropractors, plastic surgeons, nutritionists, authors, speakers, massage therapists, music instructors... The list seems endless. It doesn't much matter what industry they are in. They all have one thing in common: They had to start with active income. Every single one of them had to offer a service first, and then build on that service using the methods I teach, growing their businesses to produce the recurring income streams I describe above.

Cutting Edge Secrets of the Rich

"The good news is that, according to the Obama administration, the rich will pay for everything. The bad news is that, according to the Obama administration, you're rich."

P.J. O'Rourke

Taking your business online can be one of the smartest decisions you ever make, and not just because it will increase your exposure. Turning your business into a customer-focused lead generating machine that is capturing leads *and* auto-responding 24/7 may sound like a dream come true, but there are some principles you need to understand, or you risk wasting your time and turning potential customers off.

Here are seven secrets that not everyone will tell you about online business:

1. You've got to build a list of qualified leads (ideal clients.)

If you aren't grabbing your clients' information to keep in touch with them, you are completely wasting your time, energy, and money maintaining your site or blog. You can't assume your potential customers will remember who you are and what you do ...even supposing they actually find and visit your blog or website in the first place.

You will need to use an auto-responder service to collect their information and generate a series of follow up emails. I recommend my clients follow up and keep in touch with their "sign-ups" frequently at first, by scheduling seven emails to go out over a span of ten days, not making any offers until the last email is sent. There is a method to this madness, and it all amounts to building knowledge, goodwill, and trust. When you keep in touch with potential clients by sending them information that they will likely find highly useful, you are giving them a taste of what you're all about. If you interrupt the trust-building "dance" that takes place in those first nine days, you run a higher risk of losing their interest or trust. Statistics show that only 2% of customers will buy on the first encounter, only 3% on the second, 4% on the third …and that it takes five or more contacts to get 81% of sales.

2. Knowing a thing or two about copywriting will give you a serious advantage.

Blogs and websites are content focused, and that content has to be crafted in a way that won't turn your potential clients off. If you don't get to the point, you can lose their interest. If you can't explain what you do, you can appear unprofessional. And if you use language they don't understand, you can bore them to tears. If your first instinct is to tell your ideal clients *how* you fix water heaters instead of telling them *that* you will fix theirs fast, friendly, and cheap, then you've got a lot to learn about copywriting or should hire someone to do it for you. If you don't know how to sound compelling in your copy, or you aren't sure what exactly your customers want to read, just stop and think about what you would want to read as a customer looking at a site or blog. Customers want to hear about results and how to get solutions to their problems.

The purpose of a blog is to generate leads from Google using frequently-searched keywords, but it also has to be compelling enough to grab the attention of your ideal clients in social media. That means the post titles and headlines need to grab their attention fast. A good book to help you get your feet wet with copywriting is *Words that Sell*, by Richard Bayan.

3. Driving traffic to your blog in order to capture leads (and eventually raving fans and clients) does NOT happen without strategy.

The term "online strategy" gets thrown around a lot, but very few people really understand how important it is to have an intentional strategy, with systems set up well in advance to manage your target audience, sales funneling, email sequencing, program and product organization and delivery, customer service, marketing strategy, and customer relations.

It sounds overwhelming at first, but setting up just five necessary systems in your business can automate it to the point where it practically runs itself. Even though online marketing gurus would like you to believe that it's as easy as hitting a button on an ATM machine, your business requires a set of skills employed by a team or a very determined individual. Your online business certainly can be profitable, but for it to be profitable *sustainably*, you will want to put the proper systems in place well in advance.

4. You can double or even triple your online business by using information to create multiple income streams.

Too many small business owners fail to grow because they don't expand their product line or service offerings. One of the smartest ways to create a passive income stream is to sell information crafted and organized in such a way that your customers are buying it in downloadable form from a sales page. This passive revenue keeps your overhead low and doesn't require an investment other than the time to put it together.

5. When you offer a service or product at a higher price point, you have to realize that having a conversation with your client is inevitable.

This may sound obvious to some of you but there is a dangerous misconception, spread by many online marketers, that you can generate leads and make thousands of dollars a month very fast without talking to your customers. The sales conversation is still a *must* and even though automation is a huge advantage to the solopreneur and small business owner, it's not going to completely replace personal conversations. Having a user-friendly and easy-to-navigate website is crucial largely because you have to help lead your customers to call you, leave a message, or get on your calendar.

6. Getting the phone numbers of your potential clients will get you closer to having a conversation, which gets you closer to a sale.

Have several places on your site where your ideal customer can give you their phone number. This will make it easier for you to stay in contact with them *and* to make use of text message marketing. Mobile marketing is quickly becoming the best way to get in front of your customers. Text messages are answered over 89% of the time – much higher than email open rates. Having potential customers' phone numbers in addition to their email addresses allows you to use both of these marketing strategies, which just boosts your overall sales conversions.

7. Video is more powerful than any other form of marketing – if it's done right.

People are watching video more than they are reading, and attention spans are shrinking – often limited to a few seconds. You've got to grab their attention and get to the point fast. Video gives you several competitive advantages in your effort to engage online audiences. First, it makes them more willing to interact with your content; if they can hit a button to watch instead of read, they will. It also creates an opportunity to build up knowledge, goodwill, and trust by watching you in person rather than just reading your words. If you are able to get over being shy and are a decent communicator, you will find that including video on your site is a powerful tool that gets you closer to the sale.

Bonus: #8. Consider using a CRM system to organize your leads.

CRM stands for Customer Relationship Management system, and I see far too few people using them. A good CRM can mean the difference between struggling and making $5-20k a month. You've got to be organized with your leads and contacts because you will need to follow up with them – maybe even several times – before they will buy from you. With a CRM system like Zoho.com, you will able to take notes about potential customers and be a lot more effective at following up with them and building a relationship.

10% of Small Businesses are Getting 81% of the Sales

It's important to know a thing or two about what is really happening in sales. Your sales are crucial to your business – that shouldn't be shocking to you, but what *is* shocking is that so many small business owners are not focused on making more sales. The statistics below, taken from the book *Conquer the Chaos* by Mask and Martineau, may help you understand the importance of the follow-up.

- 2% of your potential customers will buy from you on the first contact.
- 3% will buy from you on the second contact.
- 4% will buy from you on the third contact.
- 10% will buy from you on the fourth contact.
- 81% will buy from you after the fourth contact.
- 48% of business owners will quit reaching out to their potential clients after the first contact!

If you are in business for yourself and need to increase your sales, you need to have a follow-up system in place so that you can join the 10% in getting 81% of the business.

What you focus on expands. Whether you want to increase revenue in your business or spend more time getting to know your friends on Facebook, you are always bringing more of what you focus on into your life. If your desire is a more lucrative business and you want your revenue to expand, then you most definitely want to stay focused on that, and not on albums full of pet pictures on Facebook. Below are a few ways to keep yourself focused on expanding and increasing revenue.

1. Keep a revenue tracking sheet near you to take note of each sale, each day, and each week. Your sales, revenue, and bottom line are sure to expand when you stay diligent about tracking your sales.

2. Set boundaries for yourself if you find yourself getting too distracted by Facebook, dawdling, or procrastinating – anything that takes your attention away from what you really want. Shut off Facebook and other social media distractions during the day, and only allow a few minutes of your time for things that are not directly related to income-generating activities.

3. Break down your revenue goal from your annual income goal, into weekly and then daily goals. This is a great way to help you stay focused and really causes you to engage in income-producing activities to hit that goal.

Six Secrets of Online Business

*"We women don't care too much about
getting our pictures on money as long as we
can get our hands on it."*

Ivy Baker Priest, U.S. Treasurer, 1954

Okay, so I thought it would be helpful to share a few important steps that will enlighten you and set you on the right path to creating some serious cash. Here we go:

1. Figure out what you're going to sell.

I know this may sound obvious, but you'd be surprised how many people can't decide what they actually want to sell or do or market. They need clarity. If this is you, it's okay, but nothing can happen until you decide this. Business and entrepreneurial ventures are all about filling a need and solving a problem for customers or clients. If you want to get into online business because it will keep you home with the kids or get you out of the corporate world because you can't stand it, great. However, you need to figure out how you're going to serve your clients. Who are they? What are you going to sell them, and how are you going to deliver the goods? There are many ways to reach them and information marketing is certainly a smart way to do it, but first examine some ways to deliver your service or product.

2. Marketing online needs to be consistent, strategic, and targeted.

I see so many people get sucked into thinking that some new gadget, trinket, app, or software will make their business explode. They get distracted with bells, whistles, and basically really good marketing. Most of it is useless. Using compelling marketing copy is key to good business online, but sometimes these marketing gurus use it to take advantage of entrepreneurs – especially the get-rich-quick thinkers who are inclined to waste their time, energy, and money on distractions. I've seen marketers use pink hair and crazy tattoos to get the attention of entrepreneurs who truly want to succeed, and convince them that they have to have an Alexa ranking like Facebook in order to make money. Not true! I've seen people spend crazy amounts of time on their Alexa score without making a dime. **The truth is, if you have a product or service, a marketing plan, a strategy that pulls in traffic from the right places, and a common sense approach to it all, you will make a lot of money.**

Forget about super powered buttons and plug-ins that create surges of traffic overnight. How do any of those things create income if they aren't leading people to buy something? You've got to have a plan first before you spend yourself into the ground with Google ad word classes and high-end SEO strategies. Some of the people investing in these courses aren't even ready to convert visitors into buyers yet. That's like sending a high school graduate into Orthopedic Surgery 102 before she's had a chance to take Pre-Med. The information is not going to be much use.

3. Test, track, and tweak what you do.

Even seasoned small business owners forget to do this, but the test, track, and tweak approach is the key to consistent results. Online business is very revealing. It's fairly easy to track what you are doing online, and *this information is like gold*. You get to see where your traffic is coming from, how often it's coming, and examine trends so you can keep applying the same methods (where things are going well) or switch it up and test market a new approach (in not-so-productive scenarios.)

4. Set up departments in your business as soon as possible.

Just like with any business, your online business will need to be organized into departments. You won't necessarily need to set them up in the very beginning, but the sooner the better. I coach business owners to just get started with their plan and find their clients first, but after we've established who their ideal clients are and we fill their practice to capacity, we move on to organizing departments and processes that make sense. This is when things get really fun, because once the processes are set up, hiring and delegating gives the business owner a lot more freedom and time to do what they love most.

5. Streamline your web traffic.

People often overlook this step. When you work hard to get the right traffic to your site, it's sad to realize they aren't converting. You see, people need to know what to do when they come to your site. You've got to be very simple and plain – almost direct with them. You've got to catch them and keep them. You've got to find ways to capture their attention, keep it, and grab their contact information so you can really begin the process of building a relationship and eventually earning their business. You need to have strategic places set up on your site to do this.

6. Be a sales person.

This may be a big ol' shocker for some of you, especially if you have never liked sales people. It's time to realize that sales people actually *are* the business. I know that may be hard to hear. But without sales, there is no business. No income generated, and nothing happening. That means that without someone focused on selling business, you've got yourself an *elaborate hobby*! You have to ask yourself, "Do I want a *hobby* or a *business*?" Once you have decided that you want to be a successful business owner, then you can pull your big girl boots on and realize that selling is all about relationships and service.

Five Signs You're Going to be Miserably Broke Next Month

"Money isn't everything but it ranks right up there with oxygen."

Rita Davenport

In business and in life, there are habits that prove Newton's law of motion that states that "for every action there is an equal and opposite reaction." Whether we like to admit it or not, the truth is we cause most of our own problems, uncomfortable situations, and unfortunate circumstances. Many of these situations surrounding money, profits, and revenue can be prevented. Knowing what signs to watch for and knowing what to do to prevent them is powerful.

Going broke usually throws up red flags before you actually hit that empty account, credit crunch, or cash flow standstill. Below, I've listed five warning signs and how to respond to them to avoid being miserably broke next month.

1. You aren't marketing enough.

In business, marketing has a lot to do with cash flow. Pull back on your marketing, and cash flow will pull back on you. If you have no cash flow or customers, it simply means you have not created or implemented the marketing action plan. Ad and marketing dollars are necessary but usually limited with start-ups, so it's a tricky juggling act when you are in the beginning stages, without capital or funding. It's also easy to become lackadaisical with your marketing efforts when you are consumed with serving your clients' needs. It's a very common mistake, too. Putting a marketing plan together in the beginning is key to avoiding periods of inactivity and painful cash flow crunches. I give my clients a Plan of Action that is heavily linked to their planned, pre-loaded marketing calendar. These days, there is an array of tools you can use to pre-load and automate your online marketing with little effort. It's best to devise a specific plan for each quarter with an emphasis on monitoring progress. This is why I always supply my clients with Test, Track & Tweak systems that will keep them on target to hit each weekly, monthly, and quarterly goal.

2. You aren't charging enough.

If you have a service-based business and are charging by the hour and chasing small jobs, you could be in for painfully slow months or − worse − no cash flow at all. Charging hourly for small jobs in the beginning to get started may be common practice for many service-based businesses, but the best way to break out of this is to create three programs or choices for your clients that each include a cluster of smaller services. So, for instance, if you are a logo designer or web professional, packaging your service with extras and/or supplemental services you know clients will benefit from is the way to go. Charging by the hour can create a cash flow crunch and will lead to uncomfortable "sticker shock" situations with clients after the work is done on a job that required more hours than you had planned. This in turn cuts into your work week and upsets other client projects. Time is money. So charge more, package your services, and save everything from careening out of control.

3. You're not monitoring cash flow and sales.

As entrepreneurs, we can only project and guesstimate future cash flow and upcoming revenue. However we can also make educated guesses by monitoring present sales, and act accordingly. Gathering information from sales staff (possibly yourself?) accounts receivable, client payment histories, and service fees will give you a fairly solid projection of what to expect so you can adjust and plan to avoid being broke next month or next quarter. It's difficult for business owners to prepare an accurate projection, but it's one of the most important things we can do. It's vital. One of the reasons the

Titanic sank was that one person did not do his job, by having a set of binoculars with him to project the trajectory toward the iceberg. Learn to look ahead so your ship doesn't sink.

4. You're not watching expenses.

There are multiple things that need to be done in any business, and that's why businesses thrive and grow by having teams focus on what they do best. Tracking expenses is a big part of the puzzle. Keeping track of expense amounts and due dates will keep you informed about your cash flow. That's why QuickBooks is so valuable for small businesses and solopreneurs. Use it!

5. Your number of slow paying or non-paying clients is growing.

Neglecting or not addressing slow or late paying clients will give you a cash crunch. Consistently ignoring them will cause you to be miserably broke in short order. You've got to be prompt about issuing invoices and stay on top of payments. *We teach clients how to treat us.* If we are too lazy or laid back about invoicing them, they will be equally laid back in making payments. Track accounts receivable to identify slow paying clients in advance and make the decision to not work with them or expect payment before work is started.

Many people are drawn to online business because they think it will be easy. It attracts the get-rich-quick mentality that's found in every walk of life and in any industry. While many people may think it's easy to make money online, that's the farthest thing from the truth. An online business is a lot of work, just like any other business.

But it does come with a *lot* more benefits in the passive income arena. It also has an amazing potential to create more income than you ever imagined. Compared to a good online business idea's ability to convert knowledge to income, a college degree is a joke. Online business can make you upwards of $250,000 a year if your strategy is right.

Just like any service based business, it relies on systems, hard work, determination, strategy, and *marketing*. Marketing is a *huge* part of any business.

Solopreneurs can find business a lot faster now from the comfort of their own home with the use of a single item: a laptop. Just as with anything, though, there's a catch. You will need to learn new skills. A lot of them. Some are people skills. This is a big part of it. You've got to learn to make sales, make connections, build a team, and know how people think.

It can be done, and once you start you'll get the hang of it. However, it's not something I would recommend to anyone without a healthy dose of Moxie and a desire and willingness to learn. It's a lot of work, but it also has serious income potential – like five-figure months – so it's worth it. This kind of income can seriously change your and your family's life.

You've got to want to learn and apply what you learn. It's a business just like any other business, and it's not for big talkers with no substance, or for procrastinators or people who aren't ready to implement the things they learn. It's not for perfectionists, wimps, whiners, or blamers either. Things can get messy, but you can't let that stop you.

Become More Captivating So You Can Reel Them In

Just be more captivating! Okay, so maybe it isn't that simple for everyone. If you've got a sea full of people with the attention span of goldfish, then you've really got to captivate them quickly if you want to get more clients. A great place to start is with titles that give them tips they can use and get immediately to the point. (Your blog title feeds Google as well, which is something else to think about.) Do some quick research and find out what people are already searching for on Google. You'll want to use a software program like TrafficTravis.com. Once you discover certain keywords that are already being searched by thousands of people every day on the web, you're already on the right track to grabbing some free traffic right away organically.

> *"The value of a man should be seen in what he gives and not in what he is able to receive."*
>
> Albert Einstein

Here are five more tips that can really get you the results you're looking for:

1. Give something of serious value away.

People want to trust you and sample a little of what you've got to offer. Debbie Fields knew this little secret back when she started her Mrs. Fields' cookie business. She was having trouble getting people to try or even notice her cookie shop until she decided to start giving them away as samples. That changed everything for her, and it can for you too. I give away all kind of goodies. I give away my audio Top Ten Income Streams immediately when clients opt in at the top of my site. Go visit my site now and grab it if you'd like: www.MoxieEntrepreneur.com.

2. Share advice and tips that give people results.

Don't be selfish or try to create artificial scarcity. Don't hold back. Actually share advice that potential customers can go and use to get results. Doing this proves that your expertise works and that you know what you're doing ...which means they're likely to come back and bring their friends. The key here is to get them to start talking about you and sharing your blog posts, name and information.

3. Break things down for people in simple terms.

Don't use jargon they won't understand. This is not a time to talk over their head or confuse them with words they won't recognize. You'll lose them. They'll hit that exit button so fast they won't even remember your website name ten seconds later. They'll be on to the next blog that talks to them on their level.

4. Use audio and video often.

If people can get a little closer to you by hitting a play button, they will. The words in your blog are important because they're the words that Google algorithms read with their spiders. The video, however, is for your customers, once they get to your blog. Use your video everywhere to pull them in. Post it on YouTube and publish it in a blog post with a short and interesting paragraph or two under it. Now you're ready to post a link to your blog post on social media sites. Note that you're drawing potential clients and traffic to your blog, not your YouTube channel.

And for goodness' sake do *not* be super boring in your video. Talk to the camera like it's your friend, be as natural as possible, and make sure the content and conversation is usable, valuable, and worth sharing with others.

5. Ask them to do something at the bottom of your blog post.

Encourage them to sign up and get something for free. Tell them to grab an audio or ebook in exchange for their email. Post an image to draw their attention to the free offer.

Doing business online widens the net and helps you to attract clients from all over the world. It should be easy, right? Not so fast. If you don't know what you're doing, you can find yourself lost in a sea of competitors – either being ignored or being so annoying that you turn off potential clients.

Let me explain. Doing business online has become a lot trickier in recent years. You've got to stand out, feed Google a constant stream of online activity, and pull in prospects from your social media feed. You also need to avoid creating a low-resistance environment. Being intrusive is a great way to turn any potential client off. Rather than attempting to sell something that someone doesn't actually need, the best way to become a client magnet is to find ideal clients who are likely to need what you have to offer, and then pull them in to your website with questions and engaging conversation.

Using Social Media

Facebook and other social media outlets have created a fun and easy way to peer into the psychology of your potential clients. You don't have to be Sherlock Holmes, either. It's all right there for everyone to see. All you have to do is take a look at their profile pages to see what they like, how they engage with others, and what some of their needs are. It's crazy simple, actually.

Here are a few tips for social media engagement:

1. Post a picture and ask a question.

Pictures are quite possibly the easiest way to get people's

attention. People love sharing and hitting that Like button. Post an eye-catching picture with a question to engage conversation. Let me give you a few examples: If you are a personal trainer, you could post a picture with a question like, "Who here would like to lose 10 lbs before June 1st?" or "Who would like to know how to get six pack abs in just 5 easy minutes a day?" Easy question, and it's likely to get people's attention. Once you get some "likes" and answers, you've got their names and all kinds of information to follow up with them. I wouldn't take that as an invitation to begin bombarding them with emails, but I would definitely send them a quick note.

2. Send them a quick note telling them you'd like to gift them something.

Maybe a free personal training session or a free downloadable video that shows them the 5-minute ab crunch exercise you just mentioned in your last post that they commented on. This is a sure way to get their attention because most people like the idea of getting something for free, and it eases their resistance to being "sold." Everyone wants to sample before they buy, and if you do it in such a way that you can build knowledge, goodwill, and trust, you may just find yourself making a sale soon after.

3. Use Facebook Algorithms to boost yourself up in the rankings.

If you put up a quote with your website link or name and ask people to share it on their wall, some of them are likely to do it. Their friends will see it, and are likely to take notice because it looks like an honest referral, as opposed to a sales pitch.

4. Be proactive!

Keep a list of potential customers and go comment on what they're posting. This shows them that you are engaging, approachable, and likable. People want to do business with people they like. You never know when you are going to make someone's day by noticing how cute their baby is or meeting their need to feel heard. Grab their attention with your charm. Yep, it's called connection. Remember, people want to do business with people they like. Start being liked.

Systematize Everything in Your Business

I teach people how to create four different types of income streams in their business to achieve bigger growth and a more enjoyable life. In order to do this, I teach them to implement systems in several areas of their business. The area in which you often find the most need for good systems is marketing, and there are a lot of ways to do this online. Marketing really does take a lot of time, and if you aren't out there finding clients and converting them into sales, you won't be in business at all. The key is to create systems in your marketing so it's working for you while you're focusing on other areas of your business.

Below I share a few tips to start systematizing your marketing:

1. Use an auto-responder to collect emails from site visitors, and follow up with them.

This is a must when it comes to growing fast and making a lot more money.

2. Have calls to action everywhere on your site and blog.

When you lead people to connect with you, go to your social media page, sign up for a consultation, or buy something from you, they are more likely to do it. A confused mind never buys, and if someone becomes confused about what to do next, they will quickly leave your website and move on to something else. You've got to be constantly asking them to take quick, easy action.

3. Create passive, leveraged, and recurring income streams by selling products and programs.

Income streams come in many forms. I teach people how to create multiple income streams in their businesses to better leverage their time. For instance, you can help more people at once with a good group-based service. Active income is really just trading hours for dollars, but it's still a great way to create income fast.

The Big Bank Theory: Thinking Bigger is Easier

Thinking bigger in your business will actually create more money and time. When you start a business – especially a service based business – it's easy to pay too little attention to scalability. Let's talk about what this concept means, and how you can begin using it to make more money in your business.

It was David Joseph Schwartz who said, "Think little goals and expect little achievements. Think big goals and win big success." I would like to add to that: Thinking small is exhausting and can cause a lot of stress.

When you offer a service, you are essentially trading hours for dollars, and there is only so much time in the day. You can only do so much work, and that puts a limit on how much you can earn. You have also put yourself in a situation where you don't have enough time to market your business and take care of all the other work required to run a profitable business. You have positioned yourself to live small and never have enough time. This can lead to stress and overwork and wreak havoc on your family and social life.

When you think bigger and begin applying scalability to your business model, you begin to find relief and business growth at the same time. Here are a few tips on how to think bigger, make more money, and have more time:

1. Offer your services in a way that doesn't increase your expenses.

This may mean creating an informational product that you sell or use as a marketing tool – something that does the work for you. There are many ways to go about it, but essentially you are selling the same amount of work to more people, which can save you a ton of time. Passive income generates income without any additional effort on your part. In real estate, passive income is usually associated with owning investment properties. You can create this type of income online yourself, and create a whole new income stream. This is one way to bring scalability into your business model.

2. Expand your reach – take your business online to reach more people.

When you do this you can cast a wider net and find more clients faster and more easily. You will also find that you can become more selective and only work with those people you want to work with. Taking your business online can also mean that you can raise your prices and make more money.

3. Another effective way to grow your business fast is to hire someone to do the things you don't want to do.

If you don't have time to do the marketing it takes to grow your business, hiring it out will create that scalability fast. Consistency breeds credibility, but that isn't always easy when you are trying to do everything yourself.

Conversions are All You Need

There are essentially three specific conversions that you should focus on in your online business.

1. Traffic Conversions: when someone goes from not engaging with your business online to visiting your site. Take a look at the traffic coming to your site daily or weekly.

2. Opt-in Conversions: when a casual visitor opts to receive content from you. Keep track of sign-ups or opt-ins weekly.

3. Sales Conversions: when a potential customer becomes an actual customer. Review your sales conversions – and the sales conversations you are having – weekly.

Using the list above as a focal point, do the activities below to increase your conversions:

Test, track, and tweak what is happening on your website. What you focus on expands. When you focus on the three conversions mentioned above, you will be able to take the right actions to increase them.

Add a chat window to your site to track traffic coming to your site in real time. Chat window software from Zopim.com is easy to install. Using this along with Google Analytics will keep you on top of how much traffic you have, where visitors are coming from, and what they are doing when they are on your site. This insight into the traffic activity will help you know what to do to keep the traffic coming in. You will continue to do more of what's working and less of what's not, in terms of online marketing.

Using the information provided by Google Analytics and your chat window, prepare to buy banner ads on sites that have your ideal clients and high traffic. This is not a must at first, but it is an effective advanced strategy. Be sure to investigate the site traffic level by using Alexa.com to see if their traffic is healthy and consistent. The more traffic a site gets, the lower the Alexa ranking. For instance, Google is ranked as #1, Facebook #2, and YouTube #3.

Rinse and Repeat: A Lesson in Recurring Income

It wasn't until I discovered outside sales that I felt like I'd met my dream job. I remember thinking, *Where have you been all my life?*

One of my first outside sales jobs was working for a salon distributor that sold Paul Mitchell, Graham Webb, and a whole host of other salon products to salon owners. This was right up my alley. I was finally excited about a career for a change. I'd never had a desire to cut hair but I did love the industry, and I loved sales. Not only was I able to talk about hair products all day long, but it also gave me a reason to travel. While driving and flying, no one was micromanaging me. Working under a manager had proved too confining and left no room for creativity and freedom. It was as if my true love (freedom) met up with my glamour girl side and unleashed a brand new kind of Moxie.

Selling was second nature to me. I'd been doing it since age 6. As a girl scout, I'd only earned one honor badge, the "Whale of a Sale" badge. Little did I know it was all I needed to get everything I ever wanted in life. That "Whale of a Sale" badge was a sign. You think I'm kidding, don't you? I'm not. Sales is everything. It makes the world go around. It builds clientele that keep coming back for more products and services, and it gave me the ability to do what I love, and to do it with minimal struggle and more free time.

I remember thinking that it should be easy. Rinse and repeat, right? Not so fast. I was amazed at how many salon owners and stylists were afraid of selling. I realized that I was going to have to teach sales in order to meet my own sales goals. If the stylists and salon owners weren't fully understanding the unbelievable benefits that selling products in their salons would bring them, then I'd have to teach them.

A salesperson is a consultant. That's what I was. So, as I traveled around the state, and sometimes into other states, visiting with salon owners and selling as much product to them as possible, I came up with ways for the owners to sell more. I helped them with promotions and marketing, and even helped the stylists come up with the perfect natural-feeling sales conversations.

You may not realize this but some salons can make 50% profit off of the products they sell. That isn't the crazy part though. The stunning fact was that most of the time I had to talk these owners into investing in their own businesses, and they didn't always see it as an investment.

That is what I call Industrial Age thinking! The Industrial Age is over. **This is the Entrepreneurial Age.** We all need to know how to sell. It's one of the best skills to learn, especially for experts, specialists, and entrepreneurs. It is the only thing that will get you out of a jam and increase profits. The key, when asking for the sale, is to know what you can sell. Not everything is going to be hot, which means you really have to find those multiple streams of income so that when trends change or the economy drops, it doesn't bite you in the assets.

So many business owners out there would love the opportunity to sell a recurring product in their stores or businesses to generate hundreds or even thousands in extra income every week. But these salon owners would not always jump on the opportunity. I was selling the shampoo, conditioner, and hair spray at $6-15 a bottle wholesale, while teaching them exactly what to say to easily turn around and sell it at $12-$30 a bottle. I just couldn't fathom what they were thinking when they would reply "No, thanks."

This was *serious recurring income*. Think about it: the directions on each bottle instruct the customer to rinse and repeat! But the salon owners were not even lathering up, let alone rinsing or repeating!

It blew my mind that they would choose to struggle, with an opportunity like this sitting in front of them. I had salon owners tell me that they didn't want to sell or push products to their customers for fear it would annoy them. This is fear based thinking. Running your business on fear is self-sabotaging – a recipe for failure. It never works. It means choosing to stay small, choosing non-growth, and choosing to work hard with limited freedom. Choosing to struggle is the most common business mindset I see. It's not just in the salon; this mindset touches all small businesses and experts.

It's also linked to low self-worth. When you won't help your customer with a solution to their problem, it means you fear rejection more than you want to help them. Your low self-worth is costing you thousands of dollars a year, doing your customer a disservice, and limiting your family's resources and quality of life.

I don't know about you, ladies, but as a self-diagnosed, chronic, habitual salon consumer of tons of beauty products and pampering over my life-time, I like the convenience of buying a product while sitting in the salon chair. We all need to buy the right product for us – what better advisor than our stylist to tell us what is best for our type of hair? It's consultative selling and it's what makes recurring income for you, the stylist. Statistics show that people are more likely to stay with a stylist when they buy products from them.

If I hadn't been educated about how to take care of my hair by a previous stylist, I would have continued to sport split ends and flat, lifeless hair. I assure you, this is *not* a confidence boost, or even good for your Moxie. It's the stylist who teaches me what to buy, advises me how to use a product, and prescribes me a bottle of remedy that I remember and cherish. She's the one I go to time and time again, and she's the one I refer others to.

Remember this: Sales is education. If you fear it, it's because you don't believe in what you're doing or selling, and my suggestion is to think long and hard about continuing to do something that doesn't unleash your Moxie and make you feel like you're on fire. It's called passion. You are an expert, so be an advisor. Show your passion, teach what you know, and everyone will buy from you. This will dramatically increase your income by thousands per month, bring new customers in by word-of-mouth, and keep your favorite clients coming back for more without you doing anything but advising. It's a win/win!

When stylists would tell me that they didn't want to annoy their customers by selling them products, they were really telling me they were afraid. I say it can be even worse to have to close up shop because you can't stay in business. It's worse to not see any growth in your business. It's worse to not be able to afford a family vacation. Worse to not have the time for your children or loved ones, and worse to stand on your feet all day for wages that won't pay for the lifestyle you deserve.

It's time to start thinking like an entrepreneur in every industry and service based business. Find a need and fill it. Find the solutions for your customers' hair problems or whatever problems they may have. That's what builds lasting relationships and brings the customers back in. That's what sets you apart from the others. Think to yourself, *Am I being the 20% or the 80%? The problem or the solution?*

Provocative Things Your Clients Want to Hear You Say

Your potential clients want to know you have ideas for them. Plans. They *do not* want you to waste their time or see them as a "sale." Decide before you contact them or attempt to get their attention that you will get to know them, what they do, and how you can help them even before you have the initial conversation. Be smart. Show them that you care and that you realize it's not about you; it's about them and what you can do for them.

For years I was in sales, and I was good at it. I closed more sales than most everyone on the sales teams in four major industries, rarely missed a goal, and won numerous silly plaques, trips, contests, and techy gadgets. I did it by telling potential customers what they wanted to hear ...and meaning it. Below is a list of seven powerful things your potential clients want to hear you say.

1. "I have a great idea for you, and I know it will work. I've watched your competitors, and I think you're better. I think I've identified your ideal client, and I know how we can pull them in and get more business for you. Shall we get started?"

I refused to work with crappy clients. You know the kind: they don't pay on time, are usually rude, expect more without appreciation, and consistently want something for nothing. I was not a bottom feeder. I'm not saying I didn't want to work with the little guy or help the gal who needed my advertising services or my insurance products. But I wanted the *big* fish. I wanted the *big* deals. That meant I had to learn how to sit across from the big players and play with the big boys and girls in order to make more money and get more income. It just made sense to me to work smarter, not just harder. I had to learn what they wanted to hear, and then deliver on it. I had to investigate their industry. I had to watch their marketing and advertising campaigns and do some work before I asked for the sale. I had to say things like, "I have a great idea for you, and I know it will work. I've watched your competitors, and I think you're better. I think I've identified your ideal client, and I know how we can pull them in and get more business for you." I had to put numbers together and do my research and ask questions. I had to care, show up, and follow through with everything I said I would do. I don't waste people's time either, because I hate people wasting mine. Big players and affluent clients are busy. I had to get to the point and *never* waste anyone's time.

2. "I saw you last night. You must have recognized me, because you were staring."

Be compelling with everything you do, even in your email subject line. You've got to stand out. Fortunately, it's not difficult. If you are attempting to get in front of your client by email you've got to pay attention to the subject line you are using. Seriously; it's important. I once tried and tried to get the attention of an account I wanted, and finally decided I needed to get a little **bold**. So, I sent an email to the main decision maker with a subject line that said "I saw you last night. You must have recognized me, because you were staring." It worked. This guy was busy. I knew it, and I know how we all are with our emails. So I sent him an email that I made sure would get noticed and opened. It grabbed his attention and piqued his curiosity. It made him curious about why he may have been staring at me, and suggested that possibly he knew me. It was true, too. I had seen him in a restaurant the night before. Look, it's sales. Get creative with it! Stand out. It worked – I landed the account and it was a solid one, with consistent revenue each quarter for over two years. In fact, the company I worked for is still servicing this client.

3. "I noticed you're using _____. Can I leave you a sample of our _____ and get your opinion later?"

Notice that the only thing I'm asking for in return is an opinion.

People want to be heard. They also like free stuff. One of the best ways you can get someone's attention is to give them something. It sounds simple because it is. It's a great way to break the ice and prove you're not all about "getting something" or "making a sale." It's also an excellent way to get back in the door for a follow-up conversation. Remember, it's all about connection, and this will give you an easy way to connect with them. Just remember that consistency is credibility. So, when you do this, make sure you have a great follow-up system, or you'll just look like a flake and will be wasting time, money, and energy.

4. "I want to share a bottle of cabernet I recently brought back from Napa Valley. Want to meet me later at the Regal Beagle?"

Connection is the new currency. All you have to do is a little investigative work to find out what people like and are interested in. It's that simple. People crave attention. Sometimes it takes a while to get to know someone before you are even sure if they are a potential client for you. Heck, you may not think so after having a glass of wine with them. When you take an interest in someone – what they like, their hobbies and interests – they take notice. They crave more. They *want* to work with someone who cares. I say this a lot: People do business with people they *like*. Ask questions, make it all about them – their wants, likes, dislikes, and desires. I'm not telling you to ask creepy personal questions, but if you let the conversation go to a natural place of engagement and find a happy balance while letting them do most of the talking, you'll find that it creates a powerful sense of trust, and you'll eventually win their business. Knowing when to ask for the sale and when to hold back is something of an art.

5. "How's your daughter's first year of softball?"

When it comes to business, don't think for an instant that it's really just all about business. It's not. It's about connection and engagement. We can't forget that our clients really do mean business, but let's get in the door and get their attention by noticing that they are human. For instance, for many of us, our kids are our lives. That's why we work so hard, right? That means we will stop to talk about our kids anytime, anywhere. When you remember a potential client's kid's name, where they go to dance class, that their son is graduating from college at the top of his class, that they have identical twins with unusual hair... that potential client remembers *you*. If you think this sounds crazy or too simple then you're likely struggling in sales and have never tried it. If your sales person or department is not working for you, it's because someone is too focused on making the sale and not focused on connecting. Get connected, get engaged, and get noticed *before* trying to get the sale.

6. "Absolutely, we can get that done for you by Friday."

Like music to your customers' ears, the words "Yes" and "Absolutely" are tunes that catch their attention. These words must not be empty, however. If you even remotely fail to perform, they will backfire in a big way. Give them specific dates, promptness, and consistency, and you've just made yourself known for being reliable. Trust me, so many people are *not* reliable, it's amazing how this will make you stand out. Always doing what you say you will do shouldn't be so difficult, but it is. Want to stand out and earn respect and loyalty? Do what you say you will, when you say you'll do it. Even better is to get it done *before* the promised time. Consistency breeds credibility. When you show consistency, you are proving that you are, in fact, *the* best person to do business with.

7. "What would it take to get your business?"

Your potential customers want to be heard. They want to share their thoughts and not feel like a sales target or a number. They want to know you care, and that you're putting thought into what it will take to earn their business. When you take this approach, you will earn their respect and they will often be drawn to your boldness. Once you've asked this question, you've broken the ice and expressed your desire to *earn* their business. Now you'll have to show them that you will. Also, it's important to note that after asking a question like this, it's vital to actually listen. You may hear obstacles you will need to overcome, and how you measure up against the competition. This question will make potential clients see you as resourceful and caring. It usually isn't appropriate when first meeting someone, but it is definitely a tremendously valuable strategy.

Ten Things Entrepreneurs Do to Mess Up Their Lives

1. They waste too much time hanging around the wrong people, talking about their ideas without taking action.

There are ways to go about discussing your plans to change the world and create the next best innovative idea that's going to move the world forward in a positive way. However, sharing them at Panera Bread with someone who doesn't know the first thing about strategy, hard work, and implementation is a waste of time. There are mastermind groups and networking meetings that can help you get down to business. If you're telling your ideas to too many people who don't care or have never done much themselves, you are not likely to get any useful advice. Better to save your breath and find a group that's dedicated to giving you some constructive feedback. Time is money. If you're not sitting on a lot of cash that's making you a healthy passive income stream every day, it's time to take better care of your time. Get selfish with it. Don't hand it over to just anyone; make sure you're taking some sort of action every day.

2. They spend too much time, energy, and money on a logo design.

Decide what you're going to sell and how you're going to bring in revenue right away. Ideas are great, but they won't go anywhere without proven strategies and a business model that actually makes sense. When you decide to drop money into a pretty logo or design before you really know what your business is going to make money on or who your ideal customer really is, you could be wasting your efforts and precious money on something that will be completely different 2-3 months down the road. Trust me, if you don't really know who your ideal customer is yet, then you don't know what kind of logo will attract them. Wait until you get some traction and experience behind you in that area. For instance, let's say you want to attract women and create a logo and design with a lot of feminine colors to attract them. Then you realize that working with men is actually what you enjoy or where the money is. You could find yourself feeling torn or irritated that you spent $6k on a logo that's hot pink and outlined in flowers and hearts. Make sense? Just wait and get some clients first. Here's a revelation for you: you actually *can* get business and make sales without a logo. It's true; I've done it before!

3. They try to do it all on their own or figure it all out, without getting help from a mentor or someone who has done it themselves.

It's true – you absolutely can make money if you know what you're selling, without getting advice from a mentor or coach. However, it's unlikely you will get to the level of revenue you want to be making consistently without getting help. Not getting the help you need causes stagnation – there are so many reasons why, it would take a book to lay it all out. The most prominent reason, though, is lack of experience. You cannot reliably expect to get where you've never been, doing something you've never done. Accepting this truth can set you free. When you discover that there is no way that you will be able to achieve a different result without acquiring a new skill (so you can do something you've never done before) it changes everything in your business. The quote "The teacher appears when the student is ready" has more mystical truth to it than you might imagine. When you begin opening up your mind to something, you begin attracting the results you want. However, these results almost always come with a "give and take," meaning they usually come to you in the form of opportunities.

4. They get stuck in creative mode.

Idea people make great entrepreneurs because creativity is a must with any start-up. Marketing requires creativity, and it can help you overcome obstacles in your business. However, ideas can be like poison too. Here's what I mean: If you are unable to get your creative idea off the ground, formulate it into a set of steps called a plan and struggle with following through with the plan, you either need to get an innovator and implementer on the team, or you need some other way of establishing accountability. I see too many creatives go back into creative mode and begin working on a completely new idea because the plan gets monotonous, and they just love being creative so much that they don't realize they were just starting to get traction with their first idea. It's like watching someone set off on a trip to California from Iowa and stop, forget where they were headed, make a U-turn, scratch their head and wonder why they aren't in California yet, and then blame the weather, the traffic, or the economy. Setting a plan in place and staying on course is the only way to make progress.

5. They can't make decisions.

Way too many people suffer from an inability to make decisions. Decisions will need to be made on a daily basis – sometimes many times throughout the day. Decisions about where to spend marketing dollars, color, design, email sequencing, time management, hiring, firing, what supplier to use, what customer to take on... If decisions can't be made fast, it will show up in your life and bank account. Nothing happens without decisions being made. Period. Even bad decisions are better than no decision at all. Obviously I'm not talking about making impulsive, random decisions, but when you are faced with a decision in your business, you should be able to pull the trigger within 30 seconds. The faster you get used to this, the faster you will see results.

6. They don't hire someone to help with organization, marketing, and other things they aren't good at.

Being unorganized – whether it's with your correspondence, planning, timing, or accounting – shows up in your bottom line. Very few people can work in an unorganized way and make progress, but many entrepreneurs suffer from an inability to turn their chaos into profit, and they don't realize just how beneficial it is to hire someone who *is* good at it. They see it as an unnecessary expense instead of what it is: an investment that will pay off ten times over. *Big* mistake. Sometimes I meet entrepreneurs and small business owners who continue to do this for years because they are afraid of handing tasks off for fear of losing control. This need to control everything will only keep your business small and your problems big.

7. They don't expand their product or service, or even pay attention to what it is their clients or potential clients want.

Sometimes what your ideal clients actually want is something that you can supply, but you can't see it because you are so focused on what you yourself want your customers to buy. Creating a product suite will create income streams in your business that are likely to generate the cash flow you need. It will also help you service more clients by serving different price points and expanding your customer base. Having a plethora of products puts you in a position to leverage your time better, especially if you are a service based business.

8. They spend precious time looking for venture capital.

Your time is much better spent finding customers. I don't know why so many starting entrepreneurs think finding VC funding is easier than just finding customers, but I see it all the time. What it tells me is that they just don't know how to sell. When a start-up or entrepreneur can't sell, they really don't stand a chance of getting funding. VCs want to fund companies that are already selling products people want, because the only way to prove people want something is to sell it. This may sound like a catch-22, but just going out, finding customers, and selling your product is what will turn everything around. I have to wonder if some entrepreneurs aren't actually just trying to avoid rejection.

9. They don't start building a list of leads right away.

Every business needs a list. Lead generation is the *only* way you can start making money from nothing. In fact, you can build a list without having a product or service, learn what that list wants, and then begin creating that product or service. It may sound unconventional, but it works. In fact, it's been done for years. It's one of the most powerful ways to make money online with information, and it happens to be the fastest way to create income. Nowadays, with savvy auto-response services being so economical, easy and useful, anyone can get an opt-in box collecting emails within 24 hours. If you are not building a list of qualified leads and call yourself a small business owner or entrepreneur, you're really just a hobbyist.

10. They don't focus on income producing activities.

Producing income is the most important thing you can do in your business. There will be a ton of things that seem to be more important, but entrepreneurs who fall into these traps are in for a rude awakening. *There is nothing in your business more important than bringing in income.* Some hobbyists who are disguising themselves as entrepreneurs or business owners may believe deep down that a focus on income-producing activities is greedy. This belief is at the root of their inability to succeed and make money.

Bonus: #11. They don't define what it is that they really do.

Without a strong definition of what they do – what result they produce for their clients – they are unable to market their business effectively and therefore fail to attract business. They tend to think of attracting customers as some kind of magic or luck based on positive thinking, and never really put together a marketing plan that works. If customers don't know what you do or they don't know why you exist within a few seconds of visiting your website, reading your business card, or talking with you for 30 seconds, you need help with your marketing. It's that simple.

My Wish for You

If you apply just some of what I've shared here in this book, you'll begin to unleash the real you. The YOU that was meant to live large. To get more of what you want and to find more joy and satisfaction in your life. You'll begin to have happier relationships, a much bigger bank account, and a more fulfilled life overall. Your opportunities will grow and your limitations and pain will dissipate.

My wish is that you become fully aware that you are in control of your life destiny more than you ever realized. You can heal and grow beyond the limits you've childishly set for yourself. I want you to push the envelope. Think outside of the box. Master the art of creation and innovation. Find more joy. Love more and live larger.

Realize that your habitual focus can alter your biochemistry and lead you to get what you want – or what you don't want. It's your choice. No one else can do this for you, and no one is responsible but you. You're the artist. You're the conductor. You're the one who can turn it all around. You're the solution.

Be more intentional. Stretch your imagination. Step out in Faith. Create more income and freedom in your life. Leave a new legacy for your children. Live in abundance so you can give more and find a healthier balance in your life. Know that there is always enough for everyone, because there is. Leave scarcity thinking behind you once and for all. Spend more time with those who are important to you.

Become more of a skilled problem solver. Be that glass-half-full kind of person. Go deeper and be more specific about what you want and when it will manifest. Become more general about how it's going to arrive. Know it will come in the form of opportunities and you will face inner resistance. Fight the resistance with faith in action, and surrender to knowing that what you want is on the way. Act as if. Make the space in your life for it to come. This will let it in. Stop fighting what you really want to happen. Stop giving in to self-sabotage related to irrational fears that you've stored in your subconscious mind from early on.

Take the reins and live in faith without worry and anxiety. Put more of your attention on what you can control and less on what you cannot. Stop connecting with people at the point of misery and pain. Let go of caring what others think. Look for respect only from those you respect. (That may mean you will need to reflect on who and what you respect.)

Become more aware of those around you, and ask yourself if they want the same things you want. Are they happy or miserable? Are they Moxie, or broken and depressed? Are they gossipy and rude about people, or are they excited about ideas and what could be?

My promise:

If you do intentionally add these concepts and strategies into your life, you will be well on your way to living a Moxie life. You'll have more fun. You'll feel better emotionally and physically. You'll experience peace of mind like you've never known before. You'll inspire others and therefore attract people just like you. Your self-worth will rise, and you will value others. Others will value you. You will be more confident and people will take notice. They will value your time and services if you have a business. This will increase your bottom line. You will develop leverage and scalability, and this will create a joy within you that will shine like a beacon of hope for others. You will be making an impact in the world and feeling fulfilled. You will discover a deeper meaning and purpose. You may experience true financial freedom, and break past barriers to the kind of life you and your family want to lead.

You will become the person you were meant to be.

Want even more Moxie in your life? I'd love to connect with you further and guide you on your journey to creating a business and a life you love – one that affords you everything you ever dreamed of, and then some.

1. Sign up for the free book bonuses and you'll also get my Moxie Ezine. You'll stay empowered, with specific steps and strategies that I take to an even deeper level. If you're serious about your life and business and getting what you want, go to www.MoxieU.com and download my complimentary multiple income streams guide.

2. Love this book? I'd love to hear from you! Please email me at Support@MoxieEntrepreneur.com, and tell me how this book has helped make you more Moxie.

3. Need a coach or mentor? Working with a coach is the fastest way to success, especially if you need help finding where you're stuck and what's stopping you. Find out about my programs at www.MoxieBusinessSchool.com.